Every Broken Angel

A Southern story of silence,
shame and sacred reckoning

LORA LACEY

Copyright © 2026 by Lora Lacey
All rights reserved.

No portion of this book may be reproduced in any form without written permission from the publisher or author, except as permitted by U.S. copyright law. This book may have been edited by the author with the help of AI tools, used much like a research assistant or editor. These tools offered brainstorming ideas, organizational help, and wordsmithing suggestions, but the story, voice, and meaning are entirely the author's.

This publication is designed to provide accurate and authoritative information in regard to the subject matter covered. It is sold with the understanding that neither the author nor the publisher is engaged in rendering legal, investment, accounting or other professional services. While the publisher and author have used their best efforts in preparing this book, they make no representations or warranties with respect to the accuracy or completeness of the contents of this book and specifically disclaim any implied warranties of merchantability or fitness for a particular purpose. No warranty may be created or extended by sales representatives or written sales materials. The advice and strategies contained herein may not be suitable for your situation. You should consult with a professional when appropriate. Neither the publisher nor the author shall be liable for any loss of profit or any other commercial damages, including but not limited to special, incidental, consequential, personal, or other damages. Names, characters, places, and incidents are either the product of the author's imagination or are used fictitiously. Any resemblance to actual persons, living or dead, events, or locales is entirely coincidental.

First edition 2026

ISBN: 979-8-218-75630-7

Contents

Prologue 7

Chapter One: Unwanted Inheritance 11

Chapter Two: The Paper Daughter 17

Chapter Three: Julie 25

Chapter Four: Lena's Curse 29

Chapter Five: The Crystal Cathedral 37

Chapter Six: The Blind Who See 41

Chapter Seven: Bad Choices 45

Chapter Eight: The Wood's Colt 55

Chapter Nine: Oklahoma 59

Chapter Ten: Leavin' Love 65

Chapter Eleven: The Cows 69

Chapter Twelve: The Madras Shirt 75

Chapter Thirteen: Goodbyes 83

Chapter Fourteen: Frank 87

Chapter Fifteen: The Consequence 93

Chapter Sixteen: Going to Mississippi 97

Chapter Seventeen: The Blonde Baby 103

Chapter Eighteen: Ain't Coming Back 109

Chapter Nineteen: Sam Link 117

Chapter Twenty: The Bel-air and The Big World 125

Chapter Twenty-One: A Way to Live Decent 131

Chapter Twenty-Two: J.C. Penney 139

Chapter Twenty-Three: Devil's Elbow 147

Chapter Twenty-Four: Fade to Light 151

Epilogue 153

Acknowledgements 155

Silence is not always golden—sometimes it's guilt.

Ava High School Yearbook, 1958

Praise for Every Broken Angel

A quiet, devastating story that lingers long after the final page.

— Early Reader

Beautifully written and deeply moving—it left me wanting to know more.

— Advance Reader

I cried so much for Ruby. Haunting, restrained, and profoundly human.

— Early Reader

Lacey is an excellent writer—I couldn't put it down.

— Early Reader

Prologue

February 28, 1963

The sound didn't echo; it split the night wide open. A deep, grinding thunder that rolled across the Ozark hills like bone snapping beneath the weight of something too heavy to carry.

By the gray hush of dawn, it didn't look like a crash. It looked like a battlefield, lives torn mid-sentence. Belongings strewn like marbles across the blacktop and into the ditches: a red leather purse, its contents spilled like secrets. A gold locket with a broken chain. A crushed pack of Pall Malls nearby. A still warm Zippo lighter. A Bible flung into the grass, "Merry Christmas, 1957 – Love, Mama" scrawled inside. Clothes dangling from branches. A woman's slip caught on a fence post, pale and still like a ghost waiting to be recognized.

Miles away, people sat bolt upright in bed. Dogs howled. Chickens fluttered. Windows trembled in trailers untouched by wind. Earl Reddick, two ridges over, said the ground itself lurched. "Like the earth split in half," he whispered. "Like something left."

There were eight of them. Four in the Pontiac, four in the Chevy. Teenagers, mostly, still full of laughter, sugar heat, and the belief that nothing could touch them. They sang along with static-filled radios. They kissed like tomorrow wouldn't come. And then—

Silence.

The impact was so complete, so violent, that the two cars seemed to melt into one—metal twisted into metal, headlights crushed like bone, windshields blown out like shattered promises. One girl flew twenty feet before she landed. A boy hung half out the Pontiac, his face turned to the dirt, left leg folded wrong.

The Chevy was worse. The engine thrust through the front seat, crushing the passenger. Another boy was crumpled in the back, blood threading from the corner of his lips.

Of the four in the Chevy, only two were still breathing.

One whimpered. One gurgled through crushed lungs and a neck broken. Neither spoke. They lay in that terrible stillness, surrounded by the fractured bodies of friends and strangers.

Sirens wailed. Lights slashed the frost. Paramedics moved quickly, hands steady, faces pale. They worked on the living, covered the others with coats, blankets, whatever they could find. The air was thick with smoke and oil, but beneath it drifted something far stranger—funeral lilies, strong as if someone spilled a casket-full across the ditch.

Later, the newspapers would call it a tragedy. A curve taken too fast. Kids being careless. Bad luck. Bad road. But the ones who knew—the ones who were there, or close enough to feel the shiver in their bones—told it differently. They said time folded in on itself that night. That the road never healed. That something stayed. Grief grew like moss in the corners of people's lives. Mothers stopped singing. Stories became embellished, fathers drank before noon. Younger siblings learned to laugh softly, as if joy might wake the dead.

And one girl—far away, just a baby then—wrapped in silence and held in someone else's arms, would grow up feeling it. The darkness in the night. The ache that never softened. A longing that could not be named.

Some believed all these dreams were lost before they could grow. All that remained were quiet echoes of what might have been.

But there was one thing about dreams: They didn't die. They echoed through the quiet. They waited in the dark. And if you were still enough, they'd find their way back to you.

CHAPTER ONE

UNWANTED INHERITANCE

Ruby had never truly been wanted—not by anyone who had anything to do with her birth. From the time she could steady her steps, she felt like an intruder in her own home: soft and out of place in a world that prized calloused palms and shoulders stooped from labor. The air around her was always thick with judgment, her mother's voice sharp as a briar vine, always ready to remind her that girls were little more than dead weight.

Boys could split wood, dig fence posts, gut a deer, and kill rabbits with a stick. Girls just bled and cried and got in the way. Ruby carried that truth like a stone tucked deep in her coat pocket—always there, always dragging her down.

Her mama—Margaret, though everyone called her Millie—ran wild with her sister, red lipstick smeared at the corners of her mouth, laughter slurred and sweet, cigarette hanging from her fingers. She smelled of smoke and Shalimar—the kind that hung in a room long after she'd passed through. She fancied herself a small-town Bonnie Parker—reckless, untouchable, alive. She and her sister spent time hanging out in barrooms when they were barely double digits. Millie's people were always on the fringes—outcasts, some called them, odd others whispered. Rumor was they drifted across the Midwest, never planting roots, never welcomed. They claimed Cherokee blood one day, Choctaw the next, and carried themselves with the quiet wariness of people used to sideways glances. Folks didn't trust them, and they didn't much trust folks back.

They camped on the edge-of-town, renting falling-down houses no one else wanted, then vanished before the landlord could come knocking. That sense of not belonging clung to Millie, scratchy and stubborn—and Ruby felt it too, even if no one ever said it aloud. Millie had been desperate to claw her way out. She wanted more than hand-me-down dresses and long rides in the back of a rusted truck headed nowhere. Millie was proud to say she wasn't a hillbilly; she was from Nebraska, like in the end it really mattered.

Millie wasn't real good at making smart choices, so, when Orville came home from the war—older, shadowed eyes and rough edges, he looked like a way out. He carried the weight of foreign mud on his boots and God-knows-what in his head. Millie was underage, but Orville didn't seem to care, and she was too hungry for change to ask questions.

What he offered wasn't love, not even comfort, it was escape. And for Millie, that was enough. She may have been pregnant before she ever married Orville, and folks in Taney County knew it. They never said it plain, but gossip swirled like dust on hot wind.

And then came Ruby.

Millie liked to say that Ruby's first scream in the delivery room snuffed out what little fire she had left. That comment always left the room quiet and eyes cast down.

The home hummed with secrets. Folks whispered that Ruby wasn't Orville's child. The bloodlines in that house twisted like rusted chicken wire—impossible to follow and liable to cut you if you tried.

Orville had still been in Italy when Ruby would've been conceived, slogging through muck with a rifle and a prayer. The timing never added up. But Millie stuck to her story like bark on a tree, and no one had the cruelty—or courage—to press her face to the truth.

Still, Ruby saw the looks. The too-long pauses. The pity in their eyes. She didn't need it spelled out.

She hated Orville with a quiet, permanent burn. Never called him Daddy or Pa. Mostly just "that son of a bitch" in her head. To his face, it was just "Orville." Took respect to call someone Daddy. She had none for him. All Orville had to talk about was the big war. How he was there when Mussolini was hung, how the crowds spit on him, how he was awarded a medal for bravery. Ruby doubted any of it was true. She couldn't even imagine Orville doing anything honorable.

He didn't seem to care that she didn't call him daddy. He wasn't the type to fuss over customs. If he ever heard the bite in her voice, he never let on.

Orville couldn't read a lick, though he liked to sit at the dinner table pretending to study the newspaper, flipping pages like he understood the world—even when the headlines were upside down. Mama said it was pride. Ruby thought it was ignorance in dirty overalls.

The family liked to brag that Orville came from some kind of high bloodline—that his granddaddy was a doctor. But the truth was murkier. Dr. Enoch Amsler had no formal schooling, just a bag of roots, jars of poultice, and a knack for knowing when a fever meant death or deliverance.

Folks from three hollers rode out for his cures, trading eggs or venison for tinctures or prayers. They even called him "Doc." When he died in March of 1896, the local paper ran an obituary calling him a respected citizen. Even had a real photograph above the write-up. Said he died sweating out typhoid while tending to a sick child. Still, folks in town had colorful names for the Amsler and Birchwood families that made up that brood—sinners, heathen, devil's handmaidens. Those stories always ended with a shake of the head or a glance over the shoulder.

Milk cows turned up with their teats cut off just out of meanness. A drifter disappeared after poking around the Amsler Cave. Tools vanished from barns. Chickens too. Folks started locking their doors in daylight. They called them moonshiners or makers—not out loud, not where the law could hear. It was whispered like the benediction. Said with a dose of respect, a touch of fear. They brewed corn mash, their still cobbled together from stolen parts scavenged across Taney County. The shine came in quart jars—no labels, no caps. Just cheesecloth, twine, or rusted Mason lids. You could smell it before you saw it—smoke-corn and copper, a kiss of wood smoke from where the still hissed beneath the black gum trees. Everyone knew the brew came from a patch of land with a limestone cave off Route JJ, behind a bait shack that hadn't sold worms since '32.

The real stills were deeper in—buried under brush, behind broken-down deer stands and rusted-out car skeletons. The cave was past the creek, guarded by two hounds named Chain and Mercy. The whole place smelled half sour and half sweet and always damp. You didn't go unless you were invited. Ruby never asked questions because the answers never felt safe. She learned early on that in her family, silence wasn't just habit, it was inheritance. Shame clung to them like cockleburs in a horse tail. It made everything painful.

Ruby didn't know the whole truth about her birth or who her real father was or what happened in the cave out past the creek. But she knew enough to understand that her very existence was a kind of shadow—on Millie's name, on Orville's pride, on the family's already frayed reputation. And even though no one said it out loud, Ruby felt it in the spaces between words, in the way people looked at her like she was the punchline to a joke they weren't brave enough to tell.

That kind of knowing got inside you. It worked its way into the cracks of your spirit, curled up behind your ribs, and whispered when things got quiet.

When she said her name in a store, a classroom, or the clinic downtown, people paused—just long enough to let her know they recognized it. Sometimes they'd squint, sometimes they'd nod like they were trying to place her, and then they'd step back. Conversations died. Smiles slipped off faces. On the first day of school, when the teacher called "Ruby," there'd be a murmur, a sideways glance, and someone would whisper, "She's an Amsler."

Ruby would feel her cheeks go hot, her fists ball up under the desk. She hadn't done anything wrong, but somehow, she was always the one people walked away from. It made her angry, but worse than that, it made her tired. Tired of pretending she didn't notice. Tired of trying to stand up straighter, speak softer, and be less. Because the shame didn't come from anything she did. It was passed down like an old coat: too big, too heavy, but still expected to be worn.

Sometimes she wondered what it might feel like to belong somewhere—to walk into a room and not be stared at sideways. To be someone's daughter without needing to apologize for it.

The shame wasn't just something she carried, it was something she breathed.

CHAPTER TWO

THE PAPER DAUGHTER

By the time she was seven, Ruby was in charge of all the family's wash. Bent over a metal tub with sudsy water and a washboard, she'd wring, hang, repeat—over and over until her fingers pruned and her arms ached. She worked behind the house, where the wind caught the sheets and made them billow like sails. Sometimes she'd crawl beneath them and lie on the cool grass, hidden in the linen tunnel, pretending she was somewhere far away, soft and clean, where no one yelled, no one touched, and no one needed her for anything. Truth be told, she didn't mind the repetition. The rhythm of it gave her peace. It was the only part of her day where no one asked questions or gave orders. As long as she was out at the line, she was invisible. Safe but unseen. Alone but free.

Four more babies came after Ruby over the next five years, all boys, all with the same shock of red, frizzy hair and pale skin like Orville's. There was no mistaking it. They were treated like royalty, passed from lap to lap, their giggles celebrated like Scripture. Mama doted on them in a way Ruby had never known, soft-voiced and smiling as she wiped their mouths and cupped their cheeks. Ruby watched it all from the sidelines, her hands raw and red from scrubbing their diapers. Baby Chester was the smallest of them all—barely a year old—with a bad heart the doctors couldn't fix, even if they'd had the money to try.

Chester was there on Saturday, lying quiet in Millie's arms, and by Monday, he was in the ground behind the house, wrapped in Mama's old slip and tucked in a cardboard box. Orville hammered leftover fence slats into a cross. The boys didn't even notice, too busy roughhousing and throwing rocks at squirrels. But Ruby noticed. She saw how Mama stopped singing in the mornings, how her eyes turned glassy and far-off, how she stopped reaching for anyone. Something had gone quiet in her. Chester was the only one she'd rocked to sleep every night, the only one she'd whispered lullabies to.

Over the years, Mama and Orville tried to give away all of the boys except Jack, their favorite. Ruby imagined it was hard to lose your very favorite thing and be stuck with what was left over.

Ruby's daily chore was alright except when the boys came barreling through, their muddy feet stomping through her freshly laundered sheets, smearing stains or worse, laughing, always laughing. They did it to be mean. Ruby would bite her lip until it bled, hands clenched tight, because if she fought back, there'd be punishment. Those punishments carried a cruel, almost theatrical edge—meant not just to hurt but to humiliate and break her spirit. One of the worst was the raw rice, the sharp grains biting into her tender knees. While she stayed kneeling, she was forced to hold heavy books out to her side, arms spread like a cross.

At first she tried to grit her teeth and bear it, but the weight of the books grew heavier with every passing minute. Her shoulders screamed, her arms shook, and the rice dug deeper, leaving little dents that stayed long after she was reprieved.

"Think you some angel? Angels don't backtalk their mama," Millie would spout.

But when the wind was right and the boys were off somewhere else, Ruby could close her eyes and be gone—lost in the flapping white walls of her imagined world. Her silence was her armor.

Sometimes she swore she heard baby Chester giggling in the trees. She hoped it was true that he was happy, she knew it was way better than what he would have here.

Ruby's life was the same old thing on repeat. There were no birthday parties. Not once. No cake, no candles, no cards scrawled in crooked handwriting. The day would pass like any other—quiet, blank, ignored. She knew her birthday was in November—probably the 12th— but she hated to ask again. At the end of the day, Ruby lay flat on the thin pallet, eyes wide open, staring at the ceiling boards, moonlight sifting through the cracks. The light made the dust sparkle, turned shadows long and mean, and Ruby felt caught between two worlds—half in her bed and half out, wandering with the moon.

Christmas came with a pitiful kind of ceremony. Orville would sit in the house most of the day and bark orders. Maybe go hunt for rabbits or possums. Millie might hang a torn piece of tinsel on a tree branch and call it done. Ruby's "gifts" were always practical: a pair of too-small socks, an orange, maybe a comb wrapped in newspaper. It was the same every year, and still, somehow, she always hoped for more. Something soft. Something chosen. Something that said she was important.

She spent most of her time just shrinking back from whatever was being thrown her way, the only thing about her that refused to shrink was her hair. Coarse, red, and thick curls sprang from her head like they had a mind of their own—wild, defiant, and wholly uninterested in being tamed. Ruby wished her hair was like the blonde girl, Melissa, in the class above her. She could pop out a comb from her pocket and brush her hair clean through! When Melissa turned her head from side to side, it fell like spaghetti strands down her back. Not even the plastic comb Millie tossed at her every Christmas could make a dent in her hair. It was like trying to brush a briar patch, and Ruby eventually gave up trying. Her hair, at least, seemed to know how to take up space, even if she didn't.

Ruby had round blue eyes, soft and wide, always carrying a kind of sadness that didn't belong on a child's face. The kind of sadness that made shopkeepers glance away too quickly, that made other mothers take their children's hands and steer them toward another aisle. She made people uncomfortable, unnerved them, but she didn't know why. Tiny freckles dotted her nose and cheeks, delicate as dust. Some old woman at the hardware store called them angel kisses. Said it like a blessing, like the Lord Himself had pressed His lips to her skin. But Millie never spoke of such things. Heaven wasn't a word she used much—unless she was damning someone away from it.

The Amsler house Ruby grew up in was as tired and worn-down as the people inside it. More like a barn than a house, sunlight shining bright through the gaps in the boards, gray, unpainted wood warped by sun and rain. The porch roof sagged so low to the ground, anyone over five feet had to bend down to get in. One side was broken where Orville had put his boot through it during a drunk spell. A single step led up to the front door, which stuck in the summer and rattled in the winter.

Inside, there were just two rooms, with a kitchen tucked along the far wall—an old stove with one working burner, a chipped enamel sink that drained into a metal bucket, and cabinets that always smelled faintly of mouse urine and kerosene. There was no wallpaper, no paint. The walls were lined with old newspaper and scraps of used wrapping paper, thumbtacked and peeling, like they were trying to dress up the rot. Holes in the boards had been filled with black tar, rags, or rough-cut patches nailed in with whatever rusty nails could be found. The wind still got in and so did the cold in winter. Every time the wind blew too hard, the whole place shivered like it had a nervous condition. Ruby swore if she listened close, the house was always whispering. She would sometimes wake up to her breath puffing white in the air and hear, "I'm tired too."

The ceiling inside the house was barely six feet tall—low enough that Orville's hair almost brushed the rafters when he was sober enough to stand straight. It creaked and sagged in places like it had long since given up trying to be a real roof. The Amslers were all short, Millie barely clearing five feet in her stockings. Ruby figured God had taken one look at that house and said, "Well, better make 'em short."

Millie and Orville had the only bedroom, a narrow space walled off with mismatched quilts. The kids all slept in the main room on stained mattresses or threadbare palettes laid straight on the plank floor. Every morning, it was Ruby's first chore to stack the pallets in the corner behind the couch. Every night, she placed them back in their assigned spots across the living room floor. Over and over. When she was ten, after enough begging and one embarrassing comment from a neighbor woman, Millie finally hung a quilt from the ceiling to give her some privacy. It was patched from old shirts and feed sacks, strung up on wire between two nails, swinging slightly whenever someone walked past. It wasn't much, but it was something Ruby could call her own—a thin, fraying curtain between her and everything else. That quilt felt like a door, a wall, a prayer. For the first time in her life, Ruby could breathe without someone watching. It wasn't a bedroom, but it was space. And in that house, space was sacred.

There was no indoor plumbing. The toilet was a rickety outhouse behind the shed, full of wasps in summer and a biting stench that never quite left your nose. Orville collected old newspaper on his garbage runs so all the kids could wipe their butts. Bathing was once a week—if the weather allowed—and it followed strict order: Orville first, then Millie, then the baby on down. Naturally, Ruby was last. By the time her turn came, the water was cold and filthy, the bottom of the tub slick with the week's slime. But before she could even think about washing herself, it was her job to scrub the little ones clean, one by one, their small bodies squirming under her hands like slick fish. By the time she finished, she was so wet from their splashing around, she didn't need a bath.

Part of Ruby's responsibility was hauling water from the well and keeping the fire hot under the outdoor washtub. Her arms ached from the weight of the buckets, her hands chapped raw in winter. But no one thanked her, it was just expected. Like everything else. Her hands were spotted with soot burns from dropping a log too hard or too close to the fire.

She kept what few clothes she had folded inside old cardboard boxes that smelled of mold. There was no dresser, no closet, just a corner of the floor behind the quilt curtain where she stacked them neatly—trying to keep them clean in a house that never really was. Her shoes were hand-me-downs from Aunt Mable in California, who always meant well but never guessed the right size. Some were too small, curling Ruby's toes tight as she walked; others flopped around her feet like boats. None were ever just right. But she wore them anyway, patching holes with scraps of cloth and hoping nobody noticed the way they made her limp. Once, Aunt Mable sent Ruby a pair of Batman pajamas. Ruby was thrilled until she saw they were boy pajamas with a fly. It did dampen the excitement, but she still wore them with pride.

Ruby started school late—seven years old and already carrying the tired weight of someone twice that. They'd been out in Colorado a few months before, chasing a job for Orville that never came through. By the time they'd made it back to Missouri, Ruby was behind and barely remembered her letters and numbers. But right after Labor Day, Millie finally marched her to the little schoolhouse down by the highway and dropped her off with barely a word. No registration, no supplies, just a liver cheese sandwich wrapped in wax paper.

That first day happened to be picture day, though no one had bothered to tell Millie—or if they had, she didn't care. Ruby hadn't had a proper bath since Saturday, and now it was Wednesday. Her fingernails were black-rimmed, her arms dusty and scratched from helping Orville stack broken chairs and rusty fencing he'd hauled in from someone's curb. Her face bore a smear of something—maybe ash from the fire pit or dirt from the yard—but Millie just glanced at her, gave a sigh, and yanked a comb through the thick mess. She cinched it back with a rubber band that had once held together a bundle of newspapers.

"Good enough," Millie said, already turning away.

Aunt Hannah let Ruby borrow a pink dress from her cousin, Marla. Ruby didn't know that red-haired girls weren't supposed to wear pink. Everybody knew that—pink clashed, they said, made them look blotchy or strange. But Ruby didn't know. It had once been beautiful, that pink dress—faded now from too many washes, the color soft like the petals of a wild rose left too long in the sun. The cotton had thinned at the elbows and under the arms, and the seams had been taken in and let out again so many times the stitches wobbled like crooked teeth. The white collar, still stiff from starch, had a small, tea-colored stain near the edge, shaped almost like a thumbprint. A tiny row of mismatched buttons marched down the back—one pearl, one plastic, one hanging on by a thread.

But when Ruby slipped it on, she felt taller somehow. Lighter. Like she might be worth something after all. The puffed sleeves made her feel girlish, proper, like the girls in the week-old Sunday paper ads she liked to stare at. It didn't matter that the hem fell uneven or that her shoes didn't match. For once, she didn't look like a ragamuffin. She looked like a girl who had been sent for, like someone who belonged. She arrived at school smelling faintly of old bacon grease, hands and face still smudged. Her shoes—one tight, one loose—made a clicking sound as she climbed the steps. Inside the classroom, the other girls stared. Some giggled behind their hands. One with golden braids whispered, "That's the garbage girl," and a ripple of laughter followed. Ruby's ears burned. Orville's job was no secret—hauling off folks' trash for cash, scavenging what could be sold or fixed up. She'd ridden in the truck bed more than once, curled between busted lamps and rain-soaked mattresses.

Ruby kept her eyes down, shoulders hunched. But Mrs. Blades, the teacher, didn't laugh. She was a tall woman with steel-gray hair and a voice like warm syrup. She walked right over, knelt beside Ruby's desk, and smiled like Ruby wasn't made of secondhand things.

"Let's get you cleaned up, sweetheart," she said softly.

She led her to the back corner of the room where the water basin sat. With gentle hands, she dipped a cloth into the water and began wiping Ruby's face, then her arms, as if she were tending something fragile and valuable.

"There," she said, dabbing the last bit of grime from Ruby's cheek. "Now you shine like you're supposed to."

Ruby blinked hard to keep the tears down. No one had ever cleaned her face just to be kind. Ruby didn't smile for the school picture—she didn't dare. In fact, she only recalled smiling in a picture one time. Smiling felt too much like asking for something, and Ruby had long since learned not to do that. Besides, the rubber band in her hair was pulling so tight she was pretty sure one eyebrow was higher than the other.

When the teacher said, "Say cheese," Ruby nearly said, "What kind? Government or moldy?"—but figured that might not land her on the honor roll.

CHAPTER THREE

JULIE

The baby girl was only three months old when she disappeared from Ruby's world.

Ruby had known it would be a girl before Mama ever said so—had felt it in her bones the way some folks felt storms. After four redheaded brothers, each louder and meaner than the last, she prayed nightly for a soft, warm bundle with a laugh like bells. And when the baby came, brown-haired and bright-eyed, Ruby thought maybe, just maybe, something was turning right in the world. Her hair wasn't red like the others but a dark, curly brown, like something out of a dream.

Aunt Lena had a gift for seeing the future, and she swore she could tell a baby's sex with a crystal on a string, a secret passed down through generations. She said to hold the stone over a Mama's belly, watch it swing, and the way it moved would reveal the truth: a boy or a girl. Ruby had been itching to try it on Mama when the baby was still inside, but the only stone she could find was a rough, lumpy rock from the yard. She dangled it on a scrap of twine, but the rock just hung there, stubborn and still, like it had no idea what magic it was supposed to work. Lena pondered that it wasn't the right stone—maybe it needed moonlight or a mother's secret wish—but Ruby never got another chance to test her theory.

Mama's labor was surprisingly quick and quiet, almost like she was sneaking the baby into the world without making a fuss. She barely made a sound, her breaths soft and steady, as if she didn't want anyone to notice what was happening. The whole night moved in hushed steps, with only the faintest signs that something new had arrived—silent and secret, just like the baby herself. Orville had gone to fetch Aunt Lena, who was nearly blind but worked like she had a dozen eyes, moving with sure hands and quiet confidence. He took the boys along to their cousins' house, leaving the women to tend to Mama's labor in the dark, heavy night.

A tiny cry pierced the quiet of the room, and Aunt Lena gently placed the baby in a small wooden box lined with soft blankets, her hands careful but distant, as if she was handling something fragile and unwanted at once. She looked at Ruby and told her to fetch the glass bottle from the kitchen, fill it with cow's milk and a spoonful of sugar, and feed the baby. Mama barely touched the infant herself, as if afraid the baby carried some silent, dangerous illness, leaving Ruby to care for the tiny life with a mix of hope and heavy quiet.

Ruby lay listening to the baby's thin cry, high and hollow in the night, and she couldn't figure out why Mama wouldn't just feed it. The baby just needed a mouthful. But Mama acted like each squall was a curse laid on her. Ruby thought maybe Mama was mad at her for being born, for taking up space and breath just like Ruby did. Maybe she wanted to teach it early not to count on anyone, not even its own Mama.

Ruby took to standing over the crib just to watch her sleep. She'd rest one finger on the baby's hand and feel her tiny fingers curl around it. The baby was a quiet one, smiling more than she cried. It felt like a secret they shared—this connection. A sweetness Ruby had never tasted before. This baby didn't flinch or swat or spit. She just looked up at Ruby with wide, trusting eyes like she already knew who her real protector was. Mama said the baby wasn't smiling, that babies didn't smile that young, but Ruby saw it anyway. That little face lit up with a kind of happiness Ruby didn't understand yet, a quiet joy about things she couldn't see but desperately wished she could. Julie had the chin dimple like they all had. So, Ruby knew for sure, she was her sister. Mama hadn't told anyone the baby's name. Ruby just heard them say, "the baby." So, she named her Julie and kept it locked away safe in her head.

It didn't take long for Ruby to realize the grown-ups had different plans for Julie. They didn't speak it plain, not at first. There were just whispers and sideways looks, hushed conversations in the night.

Ruby overheard Orville on the phone once, telling someone in Texas,

"She's strong and eats well. Doesn't make a fuss."

The next day, Orville seemed in high spirits.

He even laughed at the table and said they'd finally have enough for the down payment on that land out south of town.

"A homestead of our own," he grinned, tapping ash into his plate. "All we needed was a little miracle."

Then she heard Mama's footsteps, heavy and sudden, as she walked out the door. Orville followed, cursing and furious, the sound of their yelling spilling into the night like a storm breaking loose. They fought hard in the yard, voices cracking, anger sharp enough to slice through the dark.

Ruby clapped her hands tight over her ears, trembling, terrified that the walls might burst and the noise swallow her whole. Ruby's heart hammered so fiercely it felt like it might burst right through her ribs. Fear curled tight inside her chest, twisting every thought into knots. She didn't want to see what this "miracle" really meant—didn't want to face whatever dark truth was coming next. Quickly, she crawled back onto her lumpy pallet, yanked the thin quilt over her head, and pressed her face deep into the rough fabric, just like she used to when thunderstorms rolled in and the world felt too big and loud. But the shouting still slipped through the walls—muffled, sharp, and relentless. She didn't understand what they were fighting about, but deep down, she knew it wasn't just about drunkenness or jealousy. It was something else—something big enough to scare even Mama. And if Mama was scared, what hope did Ruby have?

The next afternoon, Ruby came home from school and headed straight for the baby's box, eager to play with Julie like she always did. But the box was gone—vanished without a trace. She searched every corner of the house, peeking under tables and behind doors, then spilled outside, scanning the yard and the shed. Desperation clawed at her chest; her small hands trembled as she called Julie's name in a whisper.

No one said the word "sold," but all the family knew that Mama's sister from Texas had paid for Julie. Ruby wondered why no one offered to pay for her. Everyone in the family talked about it—how badly Ruby was treated, how sad it was.

They whispered at reunions and funerals, shaking their heads with pity in their eyes. "That poor girl," they'd say. "She's had it rough, bless her heart."

But none of them ever came. No car in the drive. No outstretched hand. Ruby knew that Julie was better off in Texas. She would get rocked and they would read her books. She might even have her own books like Ruby had seen at the school library. Julie would have new clothes and not just whatever was leftover. She might even have her own bed sitting off the ground with ruffled quilts and a doll with a fresh, clean face. Just a thousand little sorrows, sealed in silence, and a baby with brown curls, carried away to Texas like a secret no one wanted to speak again.

Months later, Ruby dreamed about Julie—but it didn't feel like her. This child in her dream had soft blonde hair that tumbled in waves and bright blue eyes that sparkled like the summer sky. She was laughing, spinning in a pink sequined tutu, light and free in a way Ruby had never felt. But the dream took a darker turn. The girl's laughter faded into silence as she listened—her face turning serious, eyes searching for something Ruby couldn't see. Ruby reached out to catch her, to hold her close, but the child slipped through her fingers like water, vanishing into the mist. When Ruby woke, the image stayed with her—so vivid it haunted her every day. The baby wasn't really Julie. Or maybe she was. Either way, she felt like someone else, entirely lost, distant, and forever out of Ruby's reach.

CHAPTER FOUR

LENA'S CURSE

Orville barely slowed the truck as he rattled into Aunt Lena's rutted drive. "Go on," he muttered.

Ruby hopped down, dust puffing around her shoes. He couldn't be bothered with her on this trip to town. Ruby was glad. On the porch, Lena sat rocking, needles clicking in her hands. She was nearly blind now, her eyes milk-blue and cloudy, but her fingers moved sure and steady, feeling the yarn like it was talking to her.

She tilted her head when Ruby's foot hit the first step.

"Girl, what's bothering you?" she asked, not seeing Ruby so much as feeling the drag in her steps.

Ruby stared at the warped porch boards. She wasn't about to say anything about the baby. Lena probably already knew anyhow.

"Nothing," she mumbled.

Lena didn't press. She patted the empty chair beside her, her hand finding it without looking.

"Come sit. You sound like your heart's fixing to fall clean out."

Ruby sat, hands locked tight between her knees. Lena's cloudy eyes never found her, but somehow, she saw her anyhow. And though Ruby held her tongue, the porch felt a little safer than it had a minute before.

Lena's house sat at the edge of a gravel road, tucked deep in the hills like it'd grew right outta the dirt. It had belonged to Orville's granddaddy Amsler. Folks said when he died of the Typhoid, he left behind a wife and a passel of young'uns with nothing but books and that house. He was the last respected Amsler, and the house still carried the ghost of what it had almost been.

The old house was a two-story, with weathered gray boards, paint long stripped by wind and time. The porch wrapped wide around the front, its wood soft and groaning underfoot, shaded by a rusted tin roof that rattled in the wind. The posts leaned like tired old men, and the screen door hung crooked, whining on its hinges. On the porch, Ruby saw the signs of Lena's quiet life: a chipped blue and white ceramic bowl full of clothespins, a rusted coffee can of mint sprouting, a basket of tangled yarn and needles resting beside a rocker cushioned with faded quilt scraps. Wind chimes made of bent silverware clinked gently in the breeze, and an old cane-backed chair sat empty in the corner. Spiderwebs clung to the porch edges, and sometimes a stray cat dozed in the shade, twitching at flies. The air smelled like woodsmoke and iron-rich dirt. Somewhere down the hill, creek mud soured the breeze, mixed with honeysuckle running wild over fenceposts. Near the door, the faint scent of mothballs always hung around.

The house wasn't pretty, but it was the kind of place where memories lingered like the smell of fried chicken. Ruby could feel those ghosts under her feet, tucked in Lena's quiet pauses.

Aunt Lena lived alone but wasn't alone in the world. Folks in the holler whispered about her foggy eyes and spirit ways. Whatever their opinion, she never went without. Family, stitched together by blood, marriage, and old debts, kept her in mind, outta both respect and a little fear. Her nephew Earl brought firewood in winter, stacking it under the lean-to without a word. His wife left biscuits and preserves in a basket, wrapped in a towel that smelled like lye soap and cedar. A cousin's boy came by weekly to patch the roof or mend screens, paid in pie or a soft word from Lena that felt like a prayer, even if he didn't believe in such. Even Orville did his part by bringing her vegetables Millie canned or treasures he found on the garbage route.

They helped her because she was kin—but also because Lena knew things. She'd midwifed their babies, brewed teas for their coughs, whispered over their fevered kids in the night. Some swore she saved their lives. Others swore if you crossed her, luck would leave you. She was the last of her kind left on that land, holding tight the old stories and the hush-hush remedies passed down from her daddy's line. So, they brought what she needed and let her be. Some called her a healer. Some called her a witch. The truth was known only to Lena herself and maybe the Spirit.

Lena paused, laid the half-finished scarf in her lap. Her cloudy eyes turned toward Ruby, a faint smile on her lips.

"You know, child," she said, soft-like, "this old house holds more stories than you could count. But there's one thing I keep tighter than my own skin."

She rocked slow, fingers resting gentle on the worn quilt in her lap. Her eyes stared off toward the tree line like she was listening to wind speak.

"My granddaddy Amsler had a big leather book, cracked and worn. Full of potions and old ways, passed down long as we been breathing," she whispered. "I've got that book now. I won't let nobody see it, not even you."

"Why not, Lena? I can keep it a secret. Besides, I can barely read anyway," Ruby said.

"It's dangerous," Lena said, voice going low. "Like fire without water."

Ruby swallowed, thinking of all she didn't know but wanted to.

"Maybe one day," Lena said, voice faraway, "you'll be ready to learn. But not yet. Not while your heart's still a carryin' shadows."

Ruby nodded slow, feeling the weight of those words settle in her bones. She wasn't sure what shadows Lena was talking about, but she suspected they weren't good ones.

She stood up and twirled around once. "Aunt Lena," she asked quietly, "What kinda recipes are in that big ol' book?"

"Depends on what you mean by recipe," Lena said, her hands still. "Some's for sickness, some's for heartache. Some's for keepin' things away that got no business bein' near."

Ruby grinned sideways. "You reckon you could tell me just one? I ain't askin' for nothin' big. Maybe just somethin' to use on my brothers when they call me Mop-Head or sit on me like I'm a stump."

Lena chuckled, deep and low. "Well, child, maybe I got somethin' for bad tempers."

She leaned close, voice dropping like they were passing secrets. "Now, if a body's got worms—belly worms that make young'uns puny—there's a way. My daddy's daddy wrote it down, but I know it by heart." She nodded sagely. "Take a pinch of dried tansy root—fresh'll make you sick if you ain't careful. Then a spoon o' tobacci, bitter as a snake's heart. Grind a spoon of peach leaves. Add black walnut hulls, ground fine—the dark ones, stains your fingers. Boil it all in water with just a dab o' molasses so they'll take it down. Give it warm when they wake and again 'fore bed. No meat or pie while they're takin' it. Best under a waning moon—drives the critters out better that way."

She gave a nod like that sealed it. "Smells like a graveyard in summer, but it'll clean a body out. Just don't overdo it, or you'll be killin' more than worms."

Ruby reckoned she might have to worm the boys herself one day. Between the scratchin', bellyachin', and the way they gobbled raw dough and licked dirt, she was certain they all had worms. She pictured holdin' their noses and pourin' Lena's bitter brew down their throats while they kicked and hollered like stuck pigs.

Aunt Lena let out a big laugh, rocking back in her chair.

"Law, you don't need to whip them boys, just worm 'em good. Heck, their meaness'll crawl right out with it!"

Ruby's eyes went wide, serious as a preacher's prayer.

Lena caught the look and waved her hand.

"Now, girl, don't you go takin' me for truth. I was jokin', you hear? Don't you dare try it. Wormin's for sick bellies, not for punishin'. Some things you laugh about so they don't weigh you down, but you don't go doin' 'em."

Ruby sat quiet and swallowed hard, still thinking on all the things she didn't know.

"One day, I will tell you everything I know," Lena repeated, "but not yet."

Ruby nodded again, quiet. She believed Lena was telling her the truth. She trusted her more than anybody.

Lena reached out and took Ruby's hand, rough, warm, and steady. "Some things," Lena said, "are meant to be protected. Even from them we love." She pushed herself up from her creaky chair, one hand gliding along the porch rail. "Sit tight, girl," she said over her shoulder. "It's hotter than the devil's skillet out here. We both could use a cold swaller."

Ruby listened to her shuffle inside, the clink of glass, the thunk of the old icebox, then the sharp scrape of the ice pick rang out like distant thunder.

Lena came back holding a cloudy glass with a jagged shard of ice floating in pale yellow. The cup was a blue metal one with ridges that sweated a lot. She handed it to Ruby like it was something fine.

"Don't gulp it, or you'll get a bellyache."

Ruby took it in both hands. The cold shocked her fingers. Ice clinked, and water drops ran down her wrist, leaving a trail through the dust on her hands. She took a sip. It was tart and sweet, lemon puckering her mouth before the sugar softened it. It tasted like sunshine ought to taste—real sunshine, not the mean kind that scorched tin roofs. Ruby sat cross-legged, chin on her knees, watching dust dance in the last gold light, Lena's rocker creaking steady beside her.

Some time passed, and Ruby whispered, "Is there a spell to make folks love you?"

Lena's chair stilled. She turned toward Ruby and knew just who she was talking about. "Well now," she said softly, "that's a mighty big ask. Mean runs deep in some folks. Might not all be their fault—but I know that don't make it hurt no less."

Ruby swallowed. "But what if I did a spell? One to make Mama talk nice. Or smile at me like she does Jack. They even gave him the Little Stink nickname. You only get a nickname when people like you."

Lena reached over and touched Ruby's shoulder. "There ain't no spell in that book that can turn a heart kind once it's gone hard."

Then she pulled a drawstring pouch from her apron, stitched from feed sack. Inside: mint, rose petals, quartz, and willow bark.

"You take this home and hang it above where you sleep. Keeps the sorrow down. Helps you rest. And when folks start bein' mean, breathe deep and say, 'It ain't mine to carry.' Say it three times."

Ruby held that pouch like it was sacred. "But will it fix them?"

Lena shook her head. "No, baby girl. But it'll help fix you. And sometimes, that's the strongest spell there is."

Late into the night, Lena lay flat on her back, pinecone quilt pulled to her chin. The house breathed around her in silence, broken only by the tick of the old clock. She rolled onto her side facing the shadowed wall and let the words rise from her lips, low and certain and drawn from the old book.

"Millie, may all you deny turn to knawin' hunger in your own bones. Orville, may the battles you carry grind you to stillness until your feet find no path to walk. Spirits hear me and take these words, bind them tight to shield Ruby from their harm, and let it return whole and fierce to where it belongs."

CHAPTER FIVE

THE CRYSTAL CATHEDRAL

Ruby knew that Pap Amsler would die months before he actually did. She dreamed it a while back. Her dreams usually came true, although they came to her in riddles she couldn't always decipher. While sleeping one night in October, she heard Pap Bo say, "The truth is buried in more than dirt."

Ruby's dreams weren't dreams the way most folks knew them. The future spoke to her in symbols—a crow pecking at a blue scarf, a baby girl who never stopped crying, a burning church with no fire, and it was up to Ruby to piece them together. Dreams were sacred business, and half the time they didn't belong to her at all. They were fierce, moon-drenched hauntings that rattled her bones and left her soaked in a silence too heavy for morning. In sleep, her spirit walked out past the curtain of this world, hovering above her body, drifting through walls and crossing county lines with no map. She saw things before they happened: a cousin's stillborn baby, a flood that swelled the creek, a tornado that destroyed Mr. Stout's barn, and a man's head found near the railroad track. Grandma Land called it a gift, same as Papa Land, but Ruby wasn't sure it was. The gift came with strict rules. Mama said don't speak on it with anybody or they'll send you to the nuthouse. Ruby wasn't real sure where the nuthouse was but she was pretty certain it was better than home.

When Ruby was nine, she dreamed of a baby girl wrapped in a blanket covered in baby chicks The baby lay in the crescent of a moon, fingers tight around a blue scarf, while her golden hair shined. Ruby stood below in a field of black-eyed Susans, watching the moon rock like a cradle in the storm-washed sky. The baby didn't move or speak, but she knew her. A voice whispered, "She's yours, but she won't be yours to keep." Ruby woke crying, salt on her lips and the scent of sweat in the air. Ruby never told a soul, because it wasn't just a dream; it was a memory from the future. She would wake straight up and reach through the dark for her dream book. She would make a note on her Sayle Oil notepad, that only she could decipher.

They called Orville's father Pap. His real name was Bo Amsler, and he wasn't the kind of man who filled a room with his presence—he filled it with silence. A silence that made folks sit straighter, talk softer, and measure their words. Orville's daddy, Bo Amsler, was a bootlegger. His given name was Bo-re-gard—at least, that's how they spelled it. The best way they could. A man who never traveled more than twenty miles beyond his cave in Taney County in his whole born days, and he didn't see the need. If you couldn't find what you needed within spitting distance of your kin, you didn't need it.

Pap had the kind of face you couldn't forget but wanted to. His thin red hair clung to his scalp like a worn mop, and his saggy, heavy-lidded eyes drooped at the corners, giving him the mournful look of a hound dog that had seen too much. His skin was pale, wrinkled, and freckled, the spots faded like sun left too long on paper. Pap was short and stumpy and slouched a little, as if life had given up on tryin' to stand him straight. He wore the same pair of grease-stained and patched overalls every day, the pocket always sagging with tools and scraps of wire. Only one strap was ever buckled, because he could reach his pistol better when it wasn't. But every now and then, there'd be a piece of sugar candy tucked in there too—just one, wrapped in wax paper, and saved for Ruby. He never made a fuss about it. Wouldn't hand it to her with a smile or a wink. He'd just press it into her hand when no one was looking, usually when her daddy's back was turned. She'd close her fingers around that sweet nugget like a secret between them. And in that small, quiet gesture, she felt something that might be love.

Pap spent most of his days in the backwoods cave he'd claimed sixty years before. He called it his "stillhouse cathedral," cooking shine in copper kettles and sipping it straight from the jar like it was holy water. The law looked the other way, so long as he kept their stash full. The neighbors didn't mind; he had the best corn liquor in Taney County, and if he was successful at moonshining, he was less inclined to be out doing real evil.

Pap never had a day of school and didn't see why his six young'uns needed it either. "You don't learn a lick from books you can't learn from the woods or a man's hands," he'd bark, waving off the school bell like it was a hornet. Orville followed that line of thinking all his life—ignorance too dumb to hide. Pap Bo knew every trail through those hills, could outrun a deputy if need be. Folks came from three counties over for his shine, said it burned clean and sweet, like fire baptized. He was real particular about his mash, and his water was pure, from Bryant Creek. Nobody ever complained about mice and bugs floatin' in his liquor jars.

On New Year's Day, 1959, they found Pap Bo hanged in the limestone cathedral, swinging like a church bell. Nobody could say if it was his own rope or some else's justice. The sheriff ruled it a suicide, but nobody in the family believed it. Pap wasn't the type to tie his own noose. He was too proud and too mean. Mama said the look on his face when he was found was pure terror, not peace. Folks said he had good reason to end it, seeing how he had to go home to Grandma Amsler. Death of any kind was better than living with her.

CHAPTER SIX

THE BLIND WHO SEE

When the house got to be too much to take, Ruby would slip out the only window, bare feet on the quiet dirt path that wound around the woodshed, across the river, and through Bell Holler. She knew every bend and branch and could make it to Aunt Lena's old, crooked house before the moon was halfway overhead. Ruby ran off a lot. She was always found by Orville, one of her four brothers, or the Sheriff. She needed better hiding places or friends to help her hide, but she didn't have either.

The house stayed pitch-black, even at midday. Aunt Lena didn't bother with lights, she didn't need them. Lena would call her blinding "the accident" but she never told Ruby how it happened, and Ruby knew better than to ask. Whatever happened had left Lena with blue, foggy eyes that didn't have that black dot in the center. Her eyes looked a little like round spots of fog on the holler. She didn't bother with dark glasses or closing her eyes. She said she didn't mind how they looked, 'cause she couldn't see them.

Dark, dusty, mismatched quilts and torn lace curtains covered the windows. The house was a little cluttered, but Lena didn't own much. She moved through the house with the grace of someone who had memorized every creak in the floor, every corner of every room. When Ruby visited, she didn't need the lights either. She'd sit right on the floor beside Lena's rocker, legs pulled to her chest, letting the warm voice of the radio and Lena's quiet wisdom wrap around her like a quilt no one else could offer. Lena was only in her fifties but seemed much older, almost like she was from 1860 or some faraway time.

The old, crackling radio played near constantly, its voice a low hum in the dark. Sometimes it was country music, fiddlers from Dora, a Holiness preacher from Branson, or sometimes just static. Lena kept it going to drown out the frogs and the crickets that came alive outside as soon as the sun fell.

"Sounds like death a creepin' up," she once said, half laughing, half serious as she turned the dial just enough to muffle the sound. Them bugs remind me too much of everything I'll never see again."

The house smelled of sweet potato peelings, dried herbs, and coffee. No matter the time of day, Lena was drinking black coffee from a tin cup, off the wood stove. Ruby would sit on the floor next to Lena's rocker and talk so fast her words spilled like a waterfall—about the names kids called her, about the ache in her heart that didn't have a name. Lena never interrupted, never judged. She'd just hum now and then, nodding gently, fingers curled around her knitting that never quite became anything.

One night after Ruby had cried herself dry, she sat with her head on Lena's knee. Aunt Lena ran her fingers through Ruby's tangled curls like she was reading a story written in strands of her hair while she hummed, "Blue Moon of Kentucky."

"You think your daddy is just mean, Ruby, but that isn't all. He's cracked in ways even he don't understand," she said, soft and slow. "He was born filled too much with other folks' sorrow. Folks in this family, we pass down more than blue eyes and short tempers, we pass down all the weight that came before us. Orville's been carryin' a whole mess of ghosts for all his life."

Ruby stayed still, her eyes closed, just listening.

Lena continued, voice dipping lower, "The Amslers come from a long string of men who never fit right, men who told tall tales because the truth was too bitter. Men who'd rather fight than feel. And way back...even before you or me or Orville was thought of, there was the Birchwood-Amsel feud. That's when it really set in."

Ruby blinked, she'd heard the whispers but never the whole story.

"It started with a hog, you believe that?" Lena whispered. "Then a woman caught between the families. Before it was done, five men lay in the ground, and families didn't speak for four generations. Your great-great grandmother was an Amsler who married a Birchwood. Her family turned their backs on her like she never drew a breath. That pain... it calcified. Got handed down like a recipe no one liked but kept makin' anyway. Folks in these parts don't forget and they shore don't forgive. That's why it's always better to keep your business close and your circle small."

CHAPTER SEVEN

BAD CHOICES

That August came around, and Orville and Millie took Jack with them to south Mississippi for a job constructing the new interstate. They left the rest of the children with Aunt Hannah and Uncle Tack.

More than eighteen children and adults shared the small house. The nights were never quiet, babies crying, boys wrestling on the floorboards, someone coughing through the thin walls. But Ruby didn't mind. She could disappear into that crowd, slip off to the barn or the edge of the woods, and nobody bothered her.

In two whole years, Orville and Millie only came back to Missouri once. Ruby hated that visit, hated the way the air grew tight the minute their truck pulled up. Everyone tiptoed around the house, pretending not to hear Orville's voice cut through the rooms. Ruby had never prayed so hard for somebody to leave. When they finally drove off again, dust hanging in the road behind them, she carried the relief like a quiet secret.

Ruby acted out more and more after Julie left. At first it was little things—back talk, slamming a door, stomping barefoot down the gravel just to make someone scream. Soon it turned into sneaking out at night, skipping school, fighting with her cousins over nothing at all. She couldn't help it. Every time she opened her mouth, the wrong words tumbled out.

Every time she sat still, a restless ache made her move, even if it meant running headlong into trouble. She told herself she didn't care if they sent her off like they had Julie. Sometimes she even wished for it. Anywhere might be better than this. But then the wish would sour in her chest—what if she really was sent away? What if nobody wanted her?

School went from bad to worse. She quit turning in her work. Half the time, she wouldn't even read the questions, just stared out the window until the teacher tapped her desk with a ruler. Her grades were terrible, and more than once, the principal was beckoned to the classroom. He looked at Ruby like she was a problem he didn't know how to fix, face full of disgust and weariness.

One morning, after Ruby slapped a girl for making fun of her handwriting, the principal called her out.

"Ruby," he said, "Come on out here."

She followed, her heart thudding. He pulled out his board and said, "Bend over and grab your ankles." He gave her two licks on her bottom, firm and sharp. As bad as those two licks hurt, Ruby gritted her teeth and didn't cry, When it was over, he pulled out his handkerchief and wiped the sweat from his neck, letting out a long, tired sigh.

Ruby looked him square in the eye. "Hope you don't think that hurt," she said, voice steady.

The principal just looked at her and shook his head, "You think this is funny, but one day, the world's gonna hit back harder than I can if you don't stop all this."

By the end of the week, he called Aunt Hannah to school. Ruby sat outside while the two of them talked, hearing enough to know it wasn't a pleasant visit.

"She's just unsettled," Hannah said, low and steady. "She's been through enough. Needs patience, not threats."

The principal muttered something Ruby couldn't catch. When her aunt came out of the office, her face was worn, jaw set like stone. She didn't scold Ruby on the way home, just held her wrist tight, like she feared she might bolt and never come back.

Ruby's cousins didn't know what to make of her trouble. Some smirked, some gave a quick nervous laugh. Others just steered clear, like she had something catching. Ruby didn't bother explaining. What was there to say—that she half wanted to be sent off and half was scared to death of it? So, she kept her chin up and let them think what they wanted. Better to be called bad than dumb. Bad meant you did it on purpose. Dumb meant you couldn't help it. Ruby chose bad and wore it like a nametag, even though deep down she felt herself slipping out of everyone's reach.

Most days, she drifted off into daydreams. She wanted to go to Germany, though she only knew of it from books. She pictured herself in the Alps, living in a log cabin like Heidi, far from the noise of grown folks. In her imagination, she ran through tall grass with goats trailing behind her, red kerchief tied around her hair, air sharp and clean, nothing weighing on her shoulders.

More than anything, Ruby wanted someone to talk to. Someone who'd listen without laughing or scolding. She missed her Aunt Lena, the one who used to sit with her quietly, listening patiently. Lena lived clear on the other side of the county now, and Ruby hardly saw her. Knowing she was out there reminded Ruby that some people managed to keep a little good left in them.

Then came the new teacher, a young woman from Kansas City with her hair twisted into a bun that never seemed to come loose no matter how wild the day was. Every day, she dressed like it was school picture day, with her skirt and jacket and nice shoes. Ruby didn't understand why she tried so hard, but she was mesmerized by Miss. Cain. She had a voice that carried without shouting, and she looked every child square in the eye when she called their name, like they mattered. Ruby tried her same old tricks—slinking low in her seat, pretending she hadn't heard her name, wise cracking to cover when she didn't know the answer. But the teacher didn't flinch. She watched Ruby close, like she saw more than the noise and trouble.

One afternoon, she held Ruby back after the bell, the other kids already spilling outside. Ruby braced herself for a scolding. But the teacher sat down across from her and laid Ruby's arithmetic paper flat.

"You can do these numbers," she said softly. "But when I ask you to read the problems, you freeze." Ruby's throat closed. Nobody had ever said it plain like that before.

"I don't think you're bad," the teacher went on. "I think you just can't read like you should be able to. And that's something we can fix, if you'll let me help."

So, Ruby stayed. Ten minutes, then twenty, every day, while the teacher sounded out words slow, never once making her feel foolish. She proved that letters could be friends, not enemies. Words could open doors. Miss. Cain explained that Ruby was seeing her letters backward and not like they should be seen. Ruby felt a flicker of something she hadn't felt in a long while—maybe she could give it a try. Maybe if she worked hard, she could catch up. Then, she could even be smarter than she thought, for herself if not anyone else.

***

Ruby came through the creaking screen door of the Old Champion Store, her eyes already wandering toward things she shouldn't touch. The place smelled cool, air from the soda case mixing with the dust that drifted in from the road. She trailed along the counter, floors creaking and her eyes catching on the bright tins of gum stacked neat in rows—pink, green, and silver, shining like something meant just for her.

Her fingers twitched before her mind caught up. She told herself she was only looking, that nobody would notice one missing pack. In a blink, it was in her pocket. The tin crinkled like it was hollering her name.

"Ruby!" She froze. Cousin Jett's voice cut through the quiet, sharp and high.

"You took that gum!"

Mr. Henson turned from the register, his glasses slipping down his nose. "What's this now?" he said, eyes wide.

Ruby's stomach twisted tight. She opened her mouth to explain—to lie, maybe—but nothing came out.

The whole store fell still. The ceiling fan ticked above her, slow and steady, like it was counting the seconds until her shame settled.

By the time Aunt Hannah came in, Ruby's hands were shaking. She didn't raise her voice, didn't have to. One look was enough. Ruby set the gum on the counter, her face burning.

"I'm sorry," she whispered, though she wasn't sure who she was saying it to—Mr. Henson, Aunt Hannah, or herself. She wished she could shrink to nothing, slip through the cracks in the floorboards, and leave that moment behind forever.

***

After two weeks of punishment, Ruby was finally allowed to go into Ava with her cousins. Uncle Tack dropped them on the square before heading out to the feed store, leaving the kids to wander freely. Ruby bolted into the five-and-dime, the warm smell of popcorn and the sticky tang of the soda fountain making her chest lift with excitement. She grabbed a free bag of hot popcorn from the wagon and wandered over to the aquarium, watching the turtles lift their little heads and blink at her. She reached a finger toward the glass, imagining how soft their shells must feel, and remembered the time she'd asked Orville for a turtle—and how he had nearly lost his mind.

"Why in the hell would I pay money for somethin' that comes from a ditch?" he'd shouted, shaking his head in disbelief.

Ruby just smiled to herself, imagining the turtle she would have had if she could. Benjamin sounded like the perfect turtle name. As much as she wanted one, she had learned her lesson and knew she would never steal—no matter how tempting something might look.

Her eyes roamed the aisles. She flipped through magazines, skimming the bright covers and shiny pages, and ran her fingers along the stacks of records, imagining the music playing loud enough to make the floorboards shake. In the corner, a jukebox played a scratchy tune, its neon lights pulsing softly, while two teenagers sat at a small table, leaning close and sharing a milkshake. Ruby watched them for a moment, fascinated by how they whispered and laughed, the straws bobbing between their lips.

She peeked at the jars of candy, tempted to touch a few just to see if anyone noticed, and spun the soda-stool seats slowly, grinning at the dizzying blur. Every corner held a little treasure, and Ruby moved from one curiosity to the next, her mind buzzing with delight and wonder—but never again with the thought of taking what wasn't hers.

After the kids had fiddled with everything in the store, Mr. Norman yelled, "You're spinnin' on my stools and messin' with the shelves—get out before somethin' breaks."

All the cousins snickered and bolted for the door to make their way around the square and see what else they could get into.

Outside, a group of kids from school were hanging on the steps of the Douglas County Courthouse and sliding down the handrail. Ruby tried to cross the street before they caught a glimpse of her.

"Hey! Look who it is—Freckles!" one called, grinning. "Troublemaker, Freckles!" another shouted.

Ruby froze, heat rushing to her face. She couldn't stop herself. As fast as she could, she bolted across the street and up the hill. She grabbed the first girl she came to and yanked her pigtails, throwing her to the ground and began punching her without slowing down. Other kids yelled, backing off. Her cousins tried to pull her away, but she didn't stop until the girl was squealing, with a torn sleeve and a black eye. Ruby's chest heaved, fire simmering down. She started to cry, but wiped the tears from her face, not wanting anyone to see weakness. Her eyes fell on the spilled popcorn at her feet. Kernels scattered across the grass, and for a moment, everything froze—her fight, her fear, her frustration—caught in that tiny mess.

Just at that moment, the girl's mother stormed out of the building, pointing her finger at Ruby, face red, voice shrill. Ruby scrambled to her feet, dirt on her knees and a wild look in her eyes. The woman grabbed her daughter by the arm, shoving Ruby back.

"Don't you ever come near my girl again, you hear me?" she snapped, her voice carrying across the square.

People stopped to watch. Ruby's chest heaved and her hands shook, but she didn't back down.

"She started it," she said, her voice trembling but loud enough for everyone to hear. "She called me freckles."

The woman's face went red. "You keep your filthy mouth shut and stay away!"

Ruby blinked hard, chin lifting.

"You can call me what you want, ma'am," she said, "but I ain't the one lyin'."

With that, she turned and walked off across the square, the whispering crowd parting like water around her.

***

Later that evening, Uncle Tack staggered out, pint jar in hand, and made his way toward the field. Ruby sat on the faded-red metal hay baler, legs swinging, hands gripping the cold surface. He leaned against it, took a sip, then wiped his mouth with his sleeve.

"Mind if I sit a spell?" he asked, rough but calm.

Ruby shrugged.

"Alright then," he said, easing down beside her.

"You been runnin' yourself ragged. Ain't no reason to let every little thing push you around. You want folks to see you as smart, don't you? Don't let your temper run the show."

Ruby stayed quiet, staring at the loose hay below.

"I ain't askin' you to be perfect," he went on. "Just... try a little, Ruby. Somethin' can change if you let it."

Ruby nodded slowly, not sure she believed him, but the words planted a small seed.

***

Ruby was perched on the stairs, pretending to be busy making a clover chain, when she overheard Aunt Hannah through the kitchen window talking to Uncle Tack.

"...I don't know how they expect the kids to turn out right," Hannah said, voice tight with weariness. "Millie and Orville... they just drop them off everywhere, like the work's done once they're out of their sight. They promised they'd be back in a few months, and now..." She trailed off with a long, heavy sigh. "I'm worn out, Tack. I can't keep doing this alone."

Tack grunted, then said firmly, "They'll be back soon enough, I'll make sure of it."

"I just feel so bad for Ruby. I don't know how she isn't worse than she is. The way they treat her... it's not right. All they notice is the trouble they think she causes, never the good heart she's got."

In that moment, Ruby felt a quiet relief settle in her chest, mixed with a strange, new understanding. None of this was her fault. It had never been about her at all. Her parents were the problem. There was nothing she could do to fix it—she hadn't caused it—and for the first time, she understood that. Maybe this was better luck than any four-leaf clover.

Two weeks later, Tack loaded Ruby and the others into the truck with their few belongings and drove them across the county, back home. Their parents hadn't even bothered to come get their own children.

Tack glanced in the rearview mirror. "You okay, Ruby?"

She thought about his question for a second, and then she met his eyes. "I'm okay. I ain't scared."

By saying it out loud, a quiet strength settled over her. The fear that had clung to her for years loosened, and for the first time, she felt ready to face whatever came next.

CHAPTER EIGHT

THE WOOD'S COLT

A "Woods Colt"—that's what folks in the Ozarks called a child without a daddy in the picture. Meant the mother weren't worth much, and the baby even less. Ruby felt like she fit that bill, even if her daddy technically lived under the same roof.

She learned early that boys in her house could get away with anything short of murder. Her brothers spit at her, yanked her hair till her scalp burned, slapped her for nothing at all—and not one adult blinked. Wasn't tolerated—it was invisible. But if Ruby fought back, even once, Mama'd drag her into the kitchen, make her kneel on dry rice with a heavy Bible in each hand. "Hold 'em straight out," Mama would say. "God watches little girls with tempers," like it mattered none that the boys lit the fire.

It was July,1954. The heat clung like a second skin. Ruby was ten, barefoot, sunburnt, her elbows scraped from the last time she tried to run off. Her hair was a matted mess—Mama used to brush it, back before she quit caring. Now it was up to Ruby to comb out those mats and tangles. Ruby sat on her mat in the dark corner, trying to drag the comb through the thicket that'd gone to seed. She was startled by the screen door slamming.

Orville didn't say much. He never did. Just went into the kitchen, drank all the milk straight from the bottle, wiped his mouth on his sleeve, and walked back to the door, barking, "Git in," pointin' to the truck. Ruby didn't argue. She climbed up into that patchwork beast of a truck— made of parts from God knew where—and tried not to hope.

She wished he might surprise her with a cone from the Sugar Shack or a grape soda from Neely's. But the way the tires bit the gravel, she knew better.

Ruby stuck her head out the window, gulping down air, choking on dust. She wanted to ask where they was headed but knew better—Orville didn't allow questions.

About three hours later, he pulled a bologna sandwich from a crumpled brown sack. One sandwich. No offer. Mama hadn't had bologna, so he must've bought it in town. Ruby's stomach growled. She'd had one egg for breakfast—same as always—and that was long gone. Orville ate every bite but the crust, tossed it out the window for the birds.

Two more hours passed. Then the truck rattled down a gravel road near Ponca City, Oklahoma. Ruby thought maybe she'd been here before, but the memory was foggy. The sun had turned an orangy pink when the house came into view. On the porch were her mama's parents—Grandma and Grandpa Land.

Ruby loved her grandma, named after her, too. Grandpa was different. The cousins whispered about him in hay wagons—said he used to beat Grandma Land, knocked her jaw crooked over a cold biscuit once. Aunt Myrna found her crying in the chicken shed, face purple and hands shaking. No one said nothin' in the daylight.

Aunt Melene—Mama's second sister—had sixteen kids, all packed in like hogs in a pen, always something frying on the stove. Mama never got invited. She just loaded the kids up on Sundays and showed up like she belonged there. The cousins ran wild—barefoot, sticky, always hollering, always daring each other to do something dumb. Ruby loved it there.

It was out on the porch at the kid's table—elbows knocking elbows—where Ruby first heard it: "Grandpa Land knows when someone's fixin' to die," a cousin whispered through mashed potatoes. "Sees a casket floatin' down from the sky."

Ruby froze mid-chew. From then on, every cloud looked like a warning. Every creak in a board set her heart to racing.

Cliff continued, "Old folks say Papa Land's baby brother was sick with the fever when Papa was a boy. He had been helpin' his Mama by watchin' the baby. They told Grandpa to go out and take a break. He was sittin' on the porch when all the sudden a casket came a floatin' from the trees! Wasn't the only time, either. He does it all the time!" Grandpa Land had the Evil Eye. Like some mountain conjurer, he didn't even know he had power.

"He looked at our cow once, and she dried up right there," one cousin claimed. Another swore he stared too long at a baby, and it screamed for three days straight. Ruby didn't know if they were scared or proud, but no one stared too long at Grandpa. Just in case.

When Orville pulled into the drive, he didn't say nothin'. Just told Ruby, "Git out." Then he peeled off like he had somewhere better to be.

She didn't have no suitcase. No toys. No shoes. No books. Not even a comb for that wild hair. Just the old nightdress she'd slept in and a fear that stuck to her like a shadow.

"He sees a casket floatin' down from the sky when someone's about to die."

As Ruby walked up that rutted path toward Grandma and Grandpa Land's porch, the cousins' words echoed in her skull. She looked up, half-scared she might see one floatin' down just for her.

Grandma and Grandpa Land stared at the girl on their steps. They'd known something wasn't right for years. Seen the dirt caked under her nails. The bruises no one mentioned. The hollowness in her eyes. But they were old. And back then, folks didn't meddle unless it spilled into Sunday service.

They stepped off the porch, slow and stiff, walking toward her. Ruby felt like that deer she once surprised in the woods—still, quiet, afraid, but hoping just the same.

There she stood all alone in the driveway, barefooted and unsure.

Grandma reached out and wrapped an arm around her. Gave her a sideways squeeze and said, "Let's go feed you, girl."

CHAPTER NINE

OKLAHOMA

Mama said it was just for a little while, till Orville and the boys got things "sorted" out. It had been five years since he'd dropped her off. She didn't know what "things" she was talking about, but she knew that it was likely something involving her. Ruby prayed every night that "the thing" never got worked out. She never wanted to go back, and she was sure God wouldn't make her. Grandpa had told her the story about God's lambs, and she was one of them. Surely, God wouldn't lead her back to the slaughter.

She had been to school every day since she arrived in Ponca City. That wasn't how it had been in Missouri. Ruby had missed a lot of school because Mama hadn't made her go regular, said there was work to be done at home and learning wouldn't put food on the table. Besides, she didn't have time to be doing no homework, and Orville couldn't read, so that was that. Now, Ruby struggled with reading and arithmetic and hadn't moved up a level in two years. She was fourteen and still sitting in the fifth grade. The other kids called her dumb, but the truth was, she never had a fair shot to begin with.

The five years that she lived with her grandparents were the happiest of her life, even if the bedsprings squeaked. She was used to sleeping on the floor, so a real bed felt fabulous to her.

Grandma Land had given her a little book called a diary, but Ruby made it her dream book and put away her old notepad. As soon as she woke up, she wrote down her dreams in detail. She would sometimes dream the same thing for weeks at a time and even go back into a good dream the next night if she dared to. She was determined to see what was ahead for her in the future, and she believed these dreams were the key to something important.

Aunt Mara came from California to visit and brought Ruby a book about ballerinas, with pictures of girls in blue and pink tutus, twirling light as dandelion fluff. She'd sit real quiet, turning the pages slow, watching them leap and spin like they floated on air. The girls wore tiny slippers that looked soft as kitten paws, and their dresses sparkled like stars. Ruby couldn't quite understand all the fancy words inside, but she loved looking at them anyway—like watching a dream come to life right there on the page. Pirouette, arabesque, plié— she knew those were foreign words from another country, and she longed to go see the real ballerinas. Maybe one day she would travel to Paris. Sometimes, she'd try to copy the poses by putting a bunch of socks and tape on her toes so she could stand on them like the dancers. It made her feel a little bit like one of those ballerinas, even if her toes cracked and her legs were too short and stubby.

Grandma would brush Ruby's hair every night with her bone-handled brush and even put it up real pretty with pins and curls for school pictures. Ruby picked out her favorite dress that was brown and white checks with a white Peter Pan collar. She had never felt this fancy since her pink striped dress. This was so much better though, as she had a fresh bath and shoes without holes.

Grandma Land had hair like Ruby's, a wild, frizzy halo all around her head. It was thick and curly, more like the photos Ruby'd seen of Mama when she was young, back before Orville. Grandma's face was round and soft, with olive skin that caught the sun just right and full lips that looked made for laughing or telling stories. She didn't look white like Ruby or the boys; she had a different kind of color, something warm and deep. Ruby wasn't sure what she looked like exactly, just knew she carried a bit of

Lora Lacey

Grandma Land's mystery in her own skin, like a secret waiting to be told. Ruby wondered if maybe she came from one of them far-off places her teacher read about in school—like the boy in the turban who chased a lion and turned to butter. The family whispered her parents had died on the way to Missouri from Kentucky and she had been raised by her uncle. Grandma didn't talk about her family before Grandpa.

Grandma had baked Ruby her first ever birthday cake. It was white cake with white frosting. She even piped some waves around the edges. Ruby stood in the backyard by the dried cornstalks and held it with pride while the neighbor took her picture.

Evenings were for sitting cross- legged on the braided rug while the radio crackled from the side table. They would listen to The Lone Ranger or Fibber McGee and Molly. Grandma would rock slowly with her eyes closed, like she was transporting herself to another place. Sometimes she'd laugh out loud, a sharp sound like a whip snap that made Ruby laugh too.

Grandpa Land would just nod his head and say, "If that feller's tellin' the truth, I'm a three-legged possum with a law degree."

In the 1930s, Grandpa Land had worked at the steel mill, loading thick timbers into the roaring fires to keep the furnaces fed. One day, back when Mama was still a girl, a whole stack of wood slipped and came down on him, crushing his leg and wrecking his back for good. He never worked a regular job again but always made do somehow. Grandpa Land's garden stretched behind the white house like a patchwork quilt stitched by sun and sweat. He grew rows of sweet corn tall enough to whisper secrets, okra that prickled your fingers, fat red tomatoes that were eaten like apples, and bush beans so thick you would lose your hand picking them. There were always juicy watermelons that thumped like drums. Come summer, they'd sit outside in the shade, shelling purple peas into a big metal bowl while the sweet smell of honeysuckle drifted over the fence. Ruby's grandparents would sell their vegetables to people in a town. Grandpa called it "peddlin'."

Ruby's heart swelled in those moments, knees tucked under her chin, laughter in the air, the rhythm of work filling the air like music. The grownups would talk and hum, she felt in her small chest, a happiness so big it almost hurt—the kind of joy that only came when you knew exactly where you belonged. Grandpa would sing a song his papa taught him. An Indian song that nobody knew the meaning of. Oh, shapingy and sha pongo long, oh, shapingy and sha pongo long... it went on and on, the same lyrics.

The family story said Grandpa was part Indian. His jet-black hair and chiseled face made it believable. When Grandpa and Grandma moved to Oklahoma from Nebraska, he said the Ponca tribe was in his front yard the next morning to welcome them. They heard he was coming. Hard to know if that was true or wishful thinking, but he sure held on to it. It made Ruby curious to know how those Indians knew Papa was in town, he didn't even have a telephone.

Grandpa was even more superstitious than the hill folk, and he never crossed a black cat, walked under an open ladder, or swept the floor on New Year's Day. He threw salt over his shoulder like rice at a wedding. Once, on the way to Missouri to see the family, he turned around in the middle of the road halfway there and went back home, all because of a black cat. Some called it Granny Wisdom or Old Wives Tales, but Grandpa called it fact.

Grandpa stood up and said, "My head's splittin' like green wood on a wedge. I'm goin' to bed."

Ruby sat in the dim warmth of the front room, curled up on the old settee with a quilt across her knees. Rain tapped soft against the windows, and the smell of cornbread lingered in the air. Ruby watched as Grandma sat in her rocker nearby, her fingers busy with her mending, glasses low on her nose, but her eyes kept drifting to Ruby—quiet and pale, staring into the fire like she was trying to find answers in the flames. Grandma Land was a tiny lady. Not what one could call pretty, but she had a different sort of look. Her face was soft, and the skin had begun to loosen over her bones.

She made all her own clothes. Just like they came from a fancy store. She cut all her patterns from newspaper or paper from the grocery store. She could take a photograph from a magazine and copy that dress to perfection, if she had the notion for it. She made Ruby dresses that were prettier than Ruby could imagine. Especially the white one with navy polka-dots, that was her favorite.

On the dresser in Grandma and Grandpa's bedroom was a picture of her as a young girl. She had that same hair pulled back in a bun, but her face was rounder and much fuller, her lips plump and solemn, and she wore a white cotton dress with tiny inserts of lace. Ruby thought her grandma looked like the Queen of Persia, or at least a princess, sitting in that fancy wicker chair.

It was Grandma who finally broke the silence. "Bet you're wonderin' how your grandpa turned out so gentle," she said, not looking up from her needle and thread.

Ruby blinked, caught off guard, sure her Grandma was a mind-reader, but she nodded slowly. "He's just... so good to everybody. It's hard to picture him any other way."

Grandma gave a soft hum, half a sigh.

"Wasn't always like that. Back in the early days, before you were born, your grandpa drank hard. That Devil's brew had its claws in him. He'd come home mean, full of thunder. Loud. Slammed doors, cursed the air, paced like a wolf in a trap. He raised his hand to me plenty, and there were nights I slept with my Bible on my chest. When your Ma was a girl, he had an accident at the steel mill, where he stoked the fires all day. He was in constant pain after that and could barely work. It's hard on a man when he can't provide for his family."

Ruby looked at her, wide-eyed.

"One night," Grandma continued, her voice dropping low, "he came in late, stinking of whiskey, and just collapsed to the floor. I thought he'd was dead for sure. But when I got close, I saw he was cryin'. Not drunk tears—

real ones. Said he'd had a vision. Said he saw himself alone in a field, the ground cracked and burning, everything he loved gone. He heard voices cryin'—not words, just sorrow—and he knew it was the Lord showing him what was comin' if he didn't turn around."

She set the mending in her lap and looked Ruby square in the eye. "He begged me to forgive him. Right there on the floor. Said he was ashamed of what he'd been. And from that night forward, he never touched another drop. Started every morning with prayer, every evening with quiet. It was like watching a storm turn back into blue sky."

Ruby swallowed hard, her voice barely above a whisper. "I didn't know that."

Grandma reached out and laid a steady hand on Ruby's arm." People ain't born saints, baby. Sometimes it takes breaking to be made whole again."

CHAPTER TEN

LEAVIN' LOVE

The end of summer in Oklahoma felt different this year. The heat still clung to the afternoons, and the cicadas still screamed from the cottonwoods, but there was a hush beneath it all, like the land was bracing itself for goodbye. The grass had turned brittle and gold, the red dirt roads were cracked and dry, and the wind blew dust like memory across the yard. Everything was still—but not at peace.

Ruby saw Orville coming down the road before anyone else did. He wore a clean white shirt and held his hat in his hands, not like a man stopping by but like someone come to collect something long overdue. She knew before he even spoke.

"We're ready for you," he said in an eerily gentle way. "Your brothers have been asking every day. It's time, Ruby."

Orville had never spoken to Ruby so kindly and gently in her entire life, and Ruby was completely unnerved. Her heart bucked in her chest. She nodded at him, polite and quiet, then turned back toward the house. She didn't go inside. She ran.

Through the dry grass, past the porch, past the rusting tractor, and into the old barn where the air still smelled of hay and horses and the sun sliced through the boards in long, golden streaks. She climbed the ladder to the loft and curled up in the corner where the dust was thick and no one could see her cry. Her breath came fast. She didn't want to leave. Not yet. Maybe not ever.

It was Grandpa Land who found her. He didn't call her name. He just slowly climbed the ladder like he had a hundred times before, slow and steady, his boots creaking on each rung. He didn't ask why she ran—he just sat down beside her and looked out through the slats at the horizon.

"You can't run from this, Ruby," he said after a while. Ruby wiped her face with her sleeve but didn't answer. She turned her head slightly, just enough to let him know she was listening.

"Maw and I are old—too old to be raising a young one like you. All we do is sit in this house and work in the yard. You need friends and experiences that we can't give you. Shoot, I'll be sixty-eight come September. You're not leaving forever," Grandpa said, his voice soft now, fraying at the edges. "You're just going home. And home ain't a place that forgets you, Ruby. You'll carry us with you. And we'll carry you right back, every day."

The barn was quiet except for the wind rustling the old wood down below. Grandpa reached for her arm and looked her right in the eye, "Girl, remember that everybody is afraid of a bear, but don't let it stop you from picking the berries." Ruby had no idea what that meant, but if Grandpa said it, Ruby believed it. She looked at him, eyes wide and full of that same fear, but also something stronger. She took a long breath, then nodded. They climbed down together, and when she stepped out of the barn, the light hit her face just right—warm and gold and full of the season's last kindness.

Grandma handed Ruby a bag with her handmade clothes, a brush, toothpaste, a birthday photo of the three of them, her dream book, and a bag of sandwiches with a pickle. Lastly, Grandpa handed her three cold Sun Drop orange sodas, those were her favorites. Orville opened the truck door and pretended to wait patiently for her to climb inside.

Ruby settled into the truck. Orville revved the old engine; it sputtered and the gears squealed, then they pulled away, trailing dust and summer behind them, while Grandpa stood in the barn doorway with a small, proud wave.

Once Ruby left, Grandpa Land stood on the porch long after the dust from the truck had settled, his weathered hands gripping the rail like it was the only thing keeping him upright. Something deep in his chest ached—not just the usual pain in his bones but something heavier, colder.

He'd watched her go with a sick feeling twisting low in his gut, a feeling he couldn't shake. That night, he barely slept. Around midnight, he sat up in bed drenched in sweat, heart pounding like hooves against dry earth. He'd had a terrible vision. In it, Ruby stood alone in a white hallway, her coat too thin, her arms wrapped around herself. Behind her, a door shut slowly, and no one turned to help. Her face was pale, her eyes wide, not with pain but with the sorrow of being forgotten.

All his years of hard-earned wisdom couldn't stop what was coming. In the dream, he called out her name, but his voice was gone. When he woke, he stared into the darkness and whispered a prayer in the old way, the way his own grandfather had taught him. "May the rainbow always touch your shoulder, and may the Great Spirit bless you, my girl, He knew then what he didn't want to believe: Ruby was going to walk through something no girl should ever walk alone. And he'd made her go. That guilt would settle into his bones like winter, and he would never forgive himself.

CHAPTER ELEVEN

THE COWS

Four months after Orville made Ruby return to Missouri, the entire Amsler family was packed into the truck and headed back to Oklahoma. Since Orville would need a truck for work, half the kids had to ride in the back. Uncle Tack and Aunt Hannah and eight of their sixteen kids were going to live with Grandpa and Grandma Land too. Work in Missouri had dried up, and Tack heard from Grandpa about a big job near Ponca City that would bring them some real money. A new factory was being built, but there was one problem. A large, old cemetery covered the land where the factory would be. So, the two men were hired to dig up graves, move them to another location, and reset the headstones. Sometimes the men found old bones, buttons, and silver coins. Orville was quick to pocket whatever he found, but Clarence had a real bad feeling 'bout takin' from the dead. It bothered him that all these folks were being disturbed and couldn't help believing that the cemetery name was a bad joke. Eternal Rest Cemetery.

Orville would just snicker "Well, it's eternal alright, just nobody said where."

On weekends, Orville went to work with an old friend of Grandpa's to help on his dying dairy farm. It used to be a successful farm, but now the old widow man was left with a doorless barn, a few chickens, and six cows. The man's name was Jones Barker. He had been fairly well off, but when his wife died of consumption in 1946, Barker just couldn't stay afloat. Orville would muck the barn, fix fences, feed and milk the cows, and mend roofs. Barker would pay him in eggs, a little cash, and milk. What Barker had, he would gladly share, and Orville would gladly take it.

A car rolled slowly up the driveway, and Ruby squinted, trying to make out the folks in the car. The engine cut and the doors opened. Aunt Josie stepped out first, graceful and composed, followed by Uncle Bart, who adjusted his jacket as he reached for the backdoor. With careful hands, he swung it open, and a little girl about four hopped out, slightly stumbling on the gravel, her tiny steps unsteady but determined. She made a beeline straight onto the porch and right for Millie, who was in the rocker. She placed her small hand on Millie's leg, hoping for a nod or a smile. Ruby held her breath, torn between hope and fear, half expecting Millie to lift the child into her arms, but Millie's hand was quick, she brushed it off like a green fly.

"Get on, I don't know you."

Ruby's stomach sank. She'd seen Millie be mean plenty, but seeing her do it to a little one hurt her heart. She wanted to step up and help but stayed frozen, watching the girl pull back and hold her doll tighter. Ruby watched her Mama in that chair, looking all tense, and she wondered what kind of power a kid could have to make grown folks act so funny. It made her uneasy in a way she didn't like. Her mind was a whirl.

Grandma grabbed the little girl's hand and led her inside, Ruby right behind.

"Ruby," Grandma said steadily, "This is your cousin Lola. She lives in Texas."

In that second, Ruby understood it all. This had to be Julie. Jealousy and love hit her hard, and she couldn't say a word.

Grandma smiled and said, "Go find the cousins and play till we call you for lunch."

The cousins were playing their regular game of cowboys and Indians. They decided Lola was the perfect one to use as the new target. Ruby thought it was funny at first, watching Lola stumble and tumble as the boys pounced on her. But her lip began to tremble and she started to cry. So, Ruby took her aside and knelt beside her.

"I'll show you another game," a sly smile tugging at her lips. "Go call Uncle Orville an ole son of a bitch." She pointed her finger his way. "He'll think that's real funny."

She didn't think Lola would actually do it, but off she went, marching straight up to him and blurted it right out!

Orville's face turned beet red, and with fury in his voice, he shouted," You little brat!" Storming over to Aunt Josie, he demanded that she whoop that girl right now.

Aunt Josie shook her head and said, "She don't know what she's saying, one of your kids probably put her up to it."

The incident soured the rest of the day, and just after supper, the Texas family packed up and left. Later, after the house had grown quiet, Ruby lay awake, questions tumbling through her mind. She crept over to Marla, who was half asleep on her mat, and whispered,

"Who was that girl, really?"

Marla stirred, eyes heavy and tired, and murmured, "Stop asking so many questions, Ruby... just let it be."

The big fight at Grandpa Lands' started on Sunday and ended on Monday. It began over something small like it always did. One of the kids dug some chips out of the barn door, deep into the soft cedar. That barn meant more to Grandpa than any regular barn. He'd built it board by board all by himself.

Tempers were hot and patience was thin, with almost twenty people sharing a three bedroom house. Grandpa just lost his temper, stormed into the house, and found Orville sitting in his chair, feet up, with dirty boots laid out on the ottoman. Holding a small pocketknife, Grandpa asked, "Who does this belong to?"

Orville responded, "What difference does it make?

It matters because they destroyed my property with it. Do you have any respect?"

"By damn, they just boys, they ain't in the army," retorted Orville with a snicker.

With that, Grandpa turned around and headed for his bedroom closet, where he pulled out his Winchester double barrel shotgun. The entire room immediately silenced as Grandpa opened the breech with a quiet crack and confirmed it was loaded.

Then, slow and deliberate, he pointed it straight at Orville's chest and said, "Get the hell out of my house and take those kids and your wife with you."

Ruby saw a side from Grandpa's past come to life, and she couldn't blame him. Orville smarted back, "If you got a problem, old man, take it up with God, 'cause He made you live so long."

Orville gave him a long, hard stare and without breaking his gaze he said, "Pack."

By sundown, the Amslers were packed and ready to leave, but before they could head East, Orville had one more sin to commit. He circled back to the Barker dairy farm, stole the only trailer the old man had, hitched it to the truck, and loaded up all six cows. The old man's entire livelihood. Ruby watched through the back seat glass. She was silent, and she was sad, but she wasn't surprised. The only shocking part was that he didn't have each of them holding a chicken in their lap.

Orville drove the family and the stolen cows two towns over and made a deal with a man as shady as he was. Even sold him Barker's trailer. Now, with money in his pocket, Orville drove back to Missouri.

The only words he uttered were, "That was a good day's work."

A few weeks later, word came that Jones Barker had put a shotgun in his mouth and pulled the trigger, just after the Amslers left Oklahoma.

CHAPTER TWELVE

THE MADRAS SHIRT

It was obvious when someone new came to town. Even in the Ozarks, everybody knew everybody, or better yet were kin. So, when Clyde Elliott showed up in Ava, all the girls noticed. He had a cocky swagger for a thin guy, but you could tell he was all muscle. He was working at the Pontiac car dealership in the mechanic bay, changing tires and adding oil to cars. Ruby rode with Orville to town on Saturday morning to pick up a new belt for the truck that was squealing like a stuck pig.

Ruby got out to get some air. It was a December day but not as bitter cold as normal. The sun was actually shining, and it gave the hills some freshness.

She saw Clyde and Orville walk back out and watched them while they talked. She couldn't hear what they were saying, but Clyde put his hand on his forehead to shield his eyes from the sun and looked straight at Ruby. It scared her so bad she jumped right back into the truck and slammed the door.

Orville came swaggering back with a smirk on his face that she recognized.

"That's a new fella in town, from over at Willow Springs. He's about your age and don't know anybody here. Name's Clyde."

Ruby didn't respond. Orville kept talking. "Said he's stayin' out in Will Hicks' shed.

"So?" Ruby responded.

"So, maybe you ought to make nice to him. Him needin' a friend and all."

Ruby rolled her eyes, folded her legs Indian style on the worn seat, and let out a sigh of exasperation.

That was Orville's first mistake, suggesting something, anything, to Ruby. It was a guarantee that it would be screwed up as a soup sandwich. She knew that all he was worried about was what was in it for him. Orville never gave two damns about Ruby's love life.

She spoke with a frustrated tone, saying, "Are we going home or not?"

"Hold your horses, girl, and mind your tongue," Orville yelled. "The boy's bringing the belt directly."

A few minutes passed, and the boy came out with the part. Orville rolled down the window and took it from him, speaking up before he could walk away.

"Hey, Clyde, this here is Ruby, my girl."

Ruby gagged when she heard Orville try to claim her.

Clyde bent down and peered through the window. Ruby gave him a sideways look, just to be polite.

"How you doin', ma'am?" Clyde said.

"Fine," Ruby said back curtly. Ma'am? she thought, really? Who was this grease monkey trying to impress?

Orville opened his mouth and said, "Come on by the house Saturday, we gonna fry some fish."

Ruby knew there wasn't a plan to fry any fish. Now he was acting like they ran the Christian County Welcome Wagon. Orville was so pathetic and desperate to get rid of her that he was using that poor boy's empty belly to get his way.

Saturday came, and sure enough, Orville had gathered some fish. Buffalo maybe, or river cat. Couldn't know for sure. Mama said it all tasted the same when you covered it in meal. Ruby knew that was wishful thinking. She and Mama cut up five pounds of onions and potatoes to fry and mixed up some cornmeal, onions, and milk for hushpuppies. All the brothers were in the grass-bare yard fighting. Bernie had Little Bink by the neck, while Marvin was riding on Jimmy Dale's back and slapping him like a horse. It wasn't war but it wasn't play, it was just the daily routine.

Ruby hadn't really thought much about that boy Clyde since they pulled out of the shop, but she did notice he was a nice looking fella. Blonde hair and blue eyes, with Ruby beginning to think she had a "type." But she doubted it would be a poor one covered in Pennzoil and living in a shed. Lord, how desperate did Orville think she was? Whatever happened, it would not be with this boy. Orville had ruined that notion by just thinking on it first.

Just after the sun was straight up in the sky, Clyde came walking down the road, wearing Levi's and a blue and green plaid shirt. Ruby thought it didn't quite fit him. He was trying to look too city in this country place. But who was she to judge, she kept her clothes in a cardboard box.

Clyde's hair was combed neat and parted on the left side. His eyes were even bluer than she recalled, and he had dimples that she could see even when he didn't smile. He had a coolness about him that didn't begin with being an asshole.

The brothers all huddled around him to check him out and see if he could stand his own ground. You would have thought Santa just fell out of the sleigh, they were so excited. The oldest one of 'em thought he was the arm wrestling champ and told Clyde he couldn't eat unless he whooped him in a contest. Clyde just laughed under his breath and responded, "Yeah, kid, okay."

All the fish was eaten and the dishes had been washed when Orville suggested that he and Ruby take a walk down to the creek.

"Ruby, go show Clyde our river out back. Bet his daddy never owned a river."

Ruby just rolled her eyes again, if this bullshit kept up, she'd be blind by the time she was thirty. She whirled out the screen door that proudly announced that Holsum Bread was available and tromped down the steps.

***

"God, I hate that bastard," she said, blowing ahead of Clyde. "He makes me sick to my stomach. I swear to God, if I EVER get out of this holler, he will never see me again!"

Clyde was silent, just letting her blow off steam.

"He ruins my fuckin' life every single day, like it's his purpose on earth. A God-given mission! Now he's stuck me with you, like I don't have enough brothers to babysit."

Clyde didn't let her tone bother him any. He knew this wasn't about him at all. His own father, Noble, beat him regular just for fun. A man so full of mean that it exploded out of every part of him. Especially after Clyde's Mama Melba left them, takin her tattoos and two poodles with her. She took the important stuff and left behind three kids with Satan.

His Mama had remarried a couple of times and had a slew of young'uns from those unions. About five of them total he guessed. Clyde hadn't seen his Mama since she left him twelve years before. She was afraid to ever step her toe near Noble again, and God knew Noble didn't give a damn about parental visitation or any nonsense like that.

Clyde's older sister Becky had left just after their Mama did. She would write Clyde from Detroit and tell him all about the city. She up and ran off one night, not saying bye to nobody, not even Clyde. She sent Clyde some pictures of her all dressed up in nice clothes, greeting some Teamster Union men. He wasn't mad about it, he knew she would've died for certain if she'd stayed in Missouri. Now, Becky was working at a bar as a waitress and making real good money. Their Daddy Noble couldn't lay a hand on her anymore, so he took most of it out on Clyde and their baby sister. Noble was mad as hell that Clyde had left the farm. He relied on Clyde to do everything a mule would do, if they had one. From sunrise to sunset, it never ended. Fix the fences, milk the cows, butcher the hogs, plow the field, shear the sheep, rake the rows... And over and over again.

And for what? Nothing ever got better, and Clyde knew in his bones his daddy was born to fail. That was a hard thing for a man to wrap his head around. Seemed like Noble never got the message sent from somewhere outside himself.

"You ain't never gonna amount to nothin' no matter what. Do somethin' different or die doin' nothin.'"

Clyde heard a voice clear as day while he was cutting the nuts off a hog. Is this your life boy? You happy with this? He wasn't sure whose voice that was, but he saw it as divine intervention.

The next week, he packed his mama's locket, two pairs of pants, and two shirts mama had sent him and got on the Trailways bus for Branson. Now, he was sitting on a riverbank with a girl who was as mad at the world as he was. The two of them with that much fire surely would be like two roosters in the same coop.

Ruby had quieted down and was skipping rocks across the little stream that Orville called a river.

"This ain't Orville's river, you know. Nobody owns a river." She hesitated, "Why are you here, Clyde?"

***

Ruby had gotten pretty courageous recently and was full of piss and vinegar, which she intended to throw all over the world.

"You don't want me here?" he seemed shocked.

"Nope, I surely do not." She shook her head. "Not you or that awful plaid shirt."

Clyde smiled slightly and said, "Sure like a girl who speaks her mind, and it's called Madras. That's what the tag said, anyway."

Ruby took a deep breath and sighed. She felt a little bad for what she'd said. This poor boy didn't ask for the wrath of hell to come pouring down on him. He just wanted some home cooked food.

"I'm sorry," she apologized. "It's just that Orville is always pointin' and directin' and demandin' somethin' from me constant, and I am sick to death of it. Not really anything you did," she added.

"It's okay, I understand, maybe we can just start over proper," Clyde offered. He stuck out his hand as if to offer a handshake.

Ruby reached out with a half smile and said, "How do you do, nice to meet you, I'm Ruby Amsler."

That was the start of their "going steady." Clyde would walk to her house, and they would walk down the road, sometimes holding hands. Months passed, and Clyde felt like a steady boat in rippling waves. Ruby knew there wasn't what you'd call a spark between them, but they were comfortable together and shared stories about their troublesome childhoods. She would walk with Clyde to the payphone at the drugstore call his mama in Ohio. He did it once a month, it was in his budget. Ruby was impressed that he even had a budget.

Ruby would get on the line and say the same ole thing every time. "Hey, Mrs. Whitaker, How are you? Yes, I'm fine, thanks, how are the poodles?"

"Please add twenty-five cents," the operator would say. That was their cue to hang up.

Occasionally, when Clyde was short on money, he would call her collect and ask to speak to a Doris Day. She loved Doris Day and fancied herself a lookalike. But Ruby had seen her photo and she definitely was not Doris Day.

On those calls, his mama would say, "I'm sorry, you have the wrong number."

That was code for, 'Hey, son, I love you. Glad you're good. When you coming to see me, I may be having another baby, just got another divorce. We're fine and the poodles are good too, glad you got away from Noble and hopefully the ol' bastard will kick the bucket soon.'

A lot of information could be compacted into seven words if you tried hard enough.

CHAPTER THIRTEEN

GOODBYES

March was breaking out of winter when Clyde broke the news to Ruby.

She liked to come out to the Cameron Cemetery. It was a far piece from her house, but she would cut through the Assumption Abbey and watch for the Monks. She thought about stopping and asking if she could sign up. They took a vow of silence there, which sounded real good to Ruby. They just made fruitcake all day, and she hated fruitcake, but she could adjust to anything, she figured. Nobody talking or asking her anything.

The cemetery was so quiet, and she felt like she was appreciated there, visiting some old soul who didn't know where they belonged anymore. She liked to walk and read the stones, especially the ones with pictures. She would imagine their lives and wonder what awful tragedy caused them to be in the ground. The little angels were the saddest, lives cut short without even a chance, just like baby Chester. She wished Chester had a real burial and a stone like these babies.

Some of her kin were there, including the Birchwoods. Ruby never knew them but knew they were related, it said so on the stone. They had the prettiest spot of all, down at the bottom of the hill under the cedar trees. Ruby noticed every time she was there, a rust colored butterfly with a broken wing followed her around. It sure wasn't pretty, but it seemed to be begging for a ride out of that place. She felt sure it was her kin saying hello to her.

Orville and Millie weren't much for church, and her main experience with the Bible was connected to her rice punishment. The mystery of death always fascinated her. Maybe that came from Grandpa Land.

Ruby had drifted off in her imaginary world, when Clyde said, "Ruby, I'm leavin' for the Army in April."

Ruby didn't respond.

Clyde rattled on like he had prepared a speech.

"I have a chance to go away and get some education. They'll teach me mechanics and feed me and give me a salary. Plus, I can take real showers, not under a hose. I can't stay here no more. Hell, there's a war going on, and sure enough, I'll win that draft lottery. I'd rather go now and have my own say."

It wasn't like she was shocked he wasn't staying. He was still living in a shed, for Pete's sake. Clyde had more ambition than that and she knew it. He didn't go to all the risk and trouble of leaving Willow Springs to wash under some stranger's water hose.

What hurt was that he was going without her. Not even a suggestion or mention that he would come back for her.

Tears welled up in her eyes, and she couldn't get the words out. "You may get some education, and you may get a pine box!"

Clyde got quiet and said, "Ruby, when God wants me home, I'll be goin'. No matter where I am."

Ruby knew he was speaking the truth. She knew she had no control over the past and even less on her future.

"Please let me go too," she begged.

Clyde seemed irritated, "Ruby, you know I can't take you. What am supposed to do? Put you in my duffle bag?"

She knew he was right, but she couldn't see herself without him. Orville didn't send her out to do shameful things when Clyde was around. He was protecting her and didn't even know it. She had never been able to tell anyone about the things she was forced to do. She thought someone probably told him anyway, but he was never disrespectful enough to mention it.

Clyde hadn't pushed Ruby to anything sexual with him. They made out some, but it ended when it got too serious. Ruby decided that it wouldn't end that day. So, on the walk home, through the woods before the river, Ruby stopped. Clyde looked at her, questioning what was happening, and just like that, they did what they hadn't done before. Ruby wasn't sorry it happened. For the first time, she made a choice about her own body. Deep down, she hoped that would entice him to stay. Wasn't that how it was in the movies? Didn't men always fall for the woman in the end and come back full of regret?

***

On April 19th, 1961, Clyde pulled out of Norwood on a Greyhound headed for Alabama. Ruby walked with him to the station with all the strength she had. She refused to cry. This would not break her. She had been through worse.

Clyde dropped his duffle to the ground and reached into his pocket. Out came a gold, oval locket with a cursive A engraved on it. The chain was tarnished and knotted in one spot.

"It was my Mama's. All I have of hers. Doubt it's real gold anyway, but I want you to keep it safe. Might get me beat up if I carry it to Vietnam." He was smiling.

Ruby stared down at the locket. It meant more to her than anything she'd ever been given. She didn't have any words to say or tears left to cry.

"What's the A stand for?" she asked.

"I don't even know," Clyde said, shrugging.

Ruby just cleared her throat and said, "Thanks, Clyde."

She felt real bad that she didn't have a gift to give him.

He gave her a hug and kissed her cheek. "I'll write, I promise. You write me back, too."

He turned and climbed the three steps up the bus, said something to the driver, and made his way down the aisle. As the bus pulled away, it wheezed like it had the black lung, fumes drifted out the back. The diesel smell filled her mouth and burned her eyes, engine groaning and gears grinding. Ruby prayed some important part of the engine would just fall off right there and leave him stranded. At that moment, she regretted not being Catholic. She figured if she had some of those beads they used to pray, she could work some miracle. At least she could have looked up a recipe in Aunt Lena's leather book. She never was too good at planning ahead.

Clyde took a seat in the back by the window. The sun was glaring on the glass, and Ruby could barely make out his hand waving as the faded red bus pulled out of the station and sputtered down Hwy 65 toward Little Rock, taillights fading as the bus rounded the curve and made its way out of sight.

Ruby could only watch.

She had no idea how long she'd been standing in the parking lot when a man walked up and said, "Girl, do you need some help?"

Ruby turned to him slowly, staring at his inquiring eyes, and before she could stop herself, she responded, "I'm gonna need more than help."

CHAPTER FOURTEEN

FRANK

After Clyde left for the Army, Orville made a new plan for Ruby. "A real job," he called it. "Easy money," he said. "Some men are just lonely and need a pretty girl on their arm."

Then he would smirk and snort with a wheezing laugh, spit flying out with it.

When Ruby refused, he slapped her face and shoved her into the wall. Told her she would either give in or get the hell out.

Friday night, Orville walked in with a box. Inside was a red lace dress. He ordered her to get it on and fix her hair, told her she had somewhere special to go. She had a bad feeling in her gut, 'cause she knew he would never take her anywhere special. Ruby looked into the mirror, the red dress sleeve off her shoulder. This dress clearly said woman, and Ruby was sure it was speaking to someone else. She adjusted the straps and tugged at the waist, tried to stand the way she had seen other women stand, but it was just an act. She felt like a hooker, or what people said a hooker was. But worse than that, she felt like a child playing dress up. Ruby did as she was told and walked out on the porch. Orville stared at Ruby through a halo of smoke.

He growled and said, "Guess that's as good as it gets." Then he added,

"Do what you're told, and don't embarrass me."

After twenty minutes or so passed, a black Chevrolet Impala pulled into the drive. The windows were dark, and she could only see the faint glow of the radio and the slow burn of a cigarette. She glanced back at Orville, her heart pounding so hard she felt faint. Orville just nodded toward the car. Ruby slowly walked down the gravel and opened the door. A deep voice inside said, "Come on, sweetie, I been waiting for you."

***

This routine went on week after week. Orville would be knocking on her door on Sunday morning for his payday. Said he was in charge of her money and he would keep it so she didn't waste it. He'd hand her a dollar and walk off. He didn't seem to have an ounce of regret or remorse. Just a smile on his face like his pig won the state fair.

One Saturday in June, the whole family piled into Orville's rattletrap truck and headed down to the Legion Hall for the square dance. The place was buzzing like a hornet's nest, fiddlers sawing their strings near in half, drunk folks two-stepping cowboy boots and busted heels. Sweat, cigarette smoke, and cheap whiskey clung to the air so thick you could near chew it.

Ruby stood off to the side, arms crossed tight, watching the folks whirl and stumble, skirts flying and boots stomping. The women all had their hair teased up big, sprayed stiff like cotton candy with Aqua net—piled high like crowns, faces painted bright and shiny, laughing too loud over the music.

Women wore their best square-dancing skirts and boots to try and attract whatever despicable man was saddled up to the bar. Some of the women had dresses so low their chest popped out like two overfilled balloons. Ruby wondered if she would ever get her boobs in. Lena laughed and told her she was sure they'd been ordered from Sears and Roebuck and should get there anytime. Ruby always cracked up laughing at just the idea of that. Mama said all the women on her side developed slow and not to be in a rush. She was in a rush though. Ruby wanted to grow up and get out, and she was sure boobs needed to be the first step.

Orville was already half-lit, red in the face and puffed up, laughing with a couple of older men that Ruby didn't like the look of. She felt his eyes on her—that heavy stare he always gave when he was trying to wave her over, maybe hand her off. She ducked her head, turned her back, and slipped out through the screen door before he could call her name.

The night outside was still and heavy, the music drifting faint from inside. She stood there catching her breath, gravel crunching under her old Mary Janes—scuffed up and dirt-dusted from walking all over town. That's when she saw him, leaned up smooth against an old Ford truck under the edge of the lot's one busted light. He looked like he'd stepped straight out of a Hollywood movie: Brylcreem coated hair, jeans cuffed just so, black leather jacket hanging easy off his frame. A real greaser type, maybe two years older than her. Not real tall but lanky, like he still had another growth spurt in him. He lit a cigarette like he had all the time in the world, then looked her way with a crooked half-smile, like he already knew who she was. Ruby stood there a minute, heart beating up in her throat, those beat-up shoes planted in gravel and dust. She didn't smile. Didn't run either.

Ruby didn't know him, not really, but she'd heard talk. Folks said his name was Frank something from over near Vanzant. Had a reputation for being a ladies man. Had lots of girlfriends in three counties. Word was, he'd once knocked a fella's teeth clean outta his head and busted his jaw too, just for saying somethin' sideways to his little brother. They said he even had tattoos of naked women. Ruby wasn't sure she believed that. Some folks said he was trouble, but Ruby didn't see it that way. She liked the idea of a man who stood up for his own. Somebody who didn't look away or go quiet when things got hard. She wondered what that even felt like—to have somebody fight for you, not sell you off. What it'd be like to have a brother or a daddy who stood in front of you, instead of shoving you toward danger. She shifted her weight, scuffed her shoe into the gravel, eyes still locked on him while he flicked ash off his smoke like he wasn't in no rush. Maybe he was rough. Maybe he wasn't nothing good for her. But he looked steady. And steady, to Ruby, felt like a whole kind of love she'd never tasted.

He tilted his head slightly to the left, like he was gonna say something. And Ruby, for the first time that night, took a slow step forward, heart thumping like a rabbit's, when the screen door slammed behind her, loud as a shotgun. Ruby flinched, spine going stiff, breath catching in her throat.

Orville came barreling out the door, red-faced and wild-eyed, his belly pushing at his sweat-stained shirt, beer sloshing in one hand. He saw her standing there by the truck, saw the boy too, and his eyes near caught fire.

"Goddammit, Ruby!" he hollered, voice splintering through the night. "What the hell you doin' out here? You think this some damn fairytale? I told you stay where I could see you!"

She didn't move at first. Just stood frozen, like maybe if she stayed still enough, he'd disappear, or she would.

But he didn't. And sure enough, she was still there too. He stomped down off that porch, cursing with every step.

"You get back over here right now, girl, before I come drag your little ass myself! Don't you go makin' me look like a fool in front of folks!" Orville yelled, "Ain't nothin' free round here, boy."

The boy—Frank—didn't move either, just stood there leaning casual on his truck, jaw tight, eyes narrowing a little as he watched Orville storm closer. His smoke hanging from the side of his mouth.

Ruby's cheeks burned, she stared at the faded red advertisement on the truck door, Patton's U-Pick it Produce, Vanzant, Missouri. Her stomach turned over. The whole moment, the quiet and the almost, it was gone now—torn up and stomped flat under Orville's boots. She dropped her eyes, heart sinking, and turned to go, when suddenly Frank moved.

He opened the truck door slow and smooth, like he had all the time in the world, then tipped his head toward her and said real calm, "Let's ride."

Ruby didn't even hesitate. Didn't look back. Didn't wait to see Orville's face explode or hear what filthy things he'd shout next. She jumped in like it was the only thing that made sense, slammed that door shut with her breath caught hard in her throat, and before Orville could so much as reach the gravel, Frank punched the gas. The truck tore off down the road, tires kicking up rocks and dust, and Frank drove that truck like he had a meeting with God himself.

The lights from the legion faded fast in the rearview, just a smear of orange and noise behind her. And with every mile that passed, the pain in her chest cracked a little looser. Wind whipped through the window, tangling her hair, and for the first time in what felt like forever, she breathed without flinching. She didn't know where they were headed. Didn't care. Long as it was away from Orville. Away from that damn square dance. Away from everything that'd near broke her in two. She looked over at Frank, his jaw set firm, eyes on the dark road ahead, like he already knew—you didn't ask questions when someone was running from hell.

And Ruby... she just stared out that window and let the night swallow her whole.

CHAPTER FIFTEEN

THE CONSEQUENCE

When Orville finally got his hands on her the next morning after she came dragging back as the sun was rising, hair wild and clothes buttoned wrong, he nearly lost his mind. Didn't matter that she was sixteen. Didn't matter that she hadn't done nothing wrong but slip away for one single moment of peace. He met her at the door with his belt already in hand, eyes bloodshot and mouth foaming with cuss words. He beat her hard, swinging the strap across her back and arms. Called her every filthy name he could think of, spitting while he hollered. Then he grabbed her by the hair and dragged her to the corner of the kitchen, where he'd poured a pile of dry rice.

"Get down on it," he snarled. "You wanna act like a whore, you can learn to kneel like one."

She didn't cry, not out loud. She knelt on that rice for an hour, maybe longer—knees burning, eyes staring at the chipped linoleum, feeling the grains dig in like teeth. Her whole body was screaming, but she didn't make a sound. Wouldn't give him the pleasure.

The next two weeks were hell. Orville put her on restriction—extra chores, extra watching, and extra... things she didn't want to do. Work that left her hollowed out: days scrubbing until her knuckles bled. Nights she didn't speak of, not even to herself.

He kept her under thumb, locked in the house or out back hanging laundry till her arms ached. She wasn't allowed to talk to nobody, not even her friend Patsy when she came knocking.

Orville told folks Ruby had the flu. "Too weak to come out," he said with a smirk, drinking vodka and schnapps on the porch like a proud man with a sick hound in the shed.

Ruby heard the lies, she wasn't sick, just black and blue for trying to escape. Mama never defended Ruby. Not once. When Orville came home mad and smelling like moonshine, when the bruises bloomed on Ruby's arms and legs like dark flowers, Mama just looked the other way, like it wasn't her business. Like it was normal. Ruby could see it plain in her eyes, the way Mama wouldn't meet hers no matter how hard Ruby tried. Not a single glance that said, "I give a damn."

Mama kept busy in the kitchen, pretending like the house was normal, like every other neighbor on the road. Sometimes, Ruby'd catch Mama watching her outta the corner of her eye, but when their eyes met, Mama'd look away quick, all tight lips and quiet breathing. Like Ruby was some kind of trouble she wanted to forget. If Mama could have had the magic to just abracadabra Ruby away, she would have. Ruby learned real young that some folks just couldn't be counted on—even when they were supposed to be there.

Ruby missed Clyde something fierce. Most days, she found herself walking down to that car place just to see if maybe—just maybe—he'd changed his mind. Standin' by the lot, she hoped to catch a glimpse of him leaning against a truck, that steady look in his eyes. But he never showed.

Lately, Ruby hadn't been feeling right. Nausea hit her hard some days, like the whole world was spinning slow and her stomach was tied up in knots. One afternoon, Mama fixed turnip greens, smelling strong and bitter, but all Ruby could do was sit at the table, green herself, the taste turning her stomach even worse. Ruby discovered you hadn't been sick until you tried to throw up turnip greens. And then there was the other thing—she hadn't had her monthly since June. That kind of silence in her body made her head swim with worry and confusion. Mama never said a word 'bout such things. Didn't teach her like some mothers might've. She was glad she did all the wash so mama wouldn't notice there weren't soiled rags in the wash kettle.

Ruby knew deep down the things she'd been made to do and chose to do came with their own kind of consequences—ones you couldn't just wash off or hide. She laid on the edge of her narrow bed, frogs croaking like a warning outside her window. The box fan rattled in the corner, pushing around the heat but not cooling it.

Ruby knew that Mama would blame Clyde because it was easier than the truth. He would be the scapegoat throughout history. The one who defiled her and ran off. At least Clyde and Ruby had gone steady. The truth was, it couldn't be Clyde, though she desperately wanted the baby to be his because he was the only one who had ever looked at her with kindness.

Ruby decided that she needed to tell Clyde what had happened. She was sure he would help her out of this mess. She stood, slipped on her shoes, and walked out the door to town.

Ruby stepped into the Katz Drugstore and headed straight to the payphone. She reached into her red, plastic, coin purse and inserted a dime, dialing the number from memory, and heard a voice answer.

"Hello?"

"Hi, Mrs. Whitaker, it's Ruby."

"Who?" Mrs. Whitaker questioned.

"Ruby Amsler, Clyde's friend," she answered. Ruby tried to cover the mouthpiece with her hand so that nosy old ladies couldn't hear her. "Mrs. Whitaker, I need to talk to Clyde real bad. His last letter came back."

Mrs. Whitaker took a deep breath and replied, "Girl, Clyde was transferred to California."

Ruby's pounding heart was all she could hear. "Okay," she hesitated. "When you hear from him, please tell him I called."

Just as Ruby was about to replace the receiver, she heard Mrs. Whitaker clear her throat. Then, "Oh, and, Ruby—you should know, Clyde got married."

CHAPTER SIXTEEN

GOING TO MISSISSIPPI

By October, Ruby's belly had taken a different shape—round and tight and trying to claw its way out. At first she thought it was stress, or summer heat, or something she ate, but no hiding it now. She watched herself in the mirror at night, palms pressed against her belly, trying to push it back in and undo whatever had taken root.

Ruby never told her mama she was pregnant, but she caught her taking long glances at her with worried eyes. Ruby practiced how to say, "Mama, I think I'm pregnant," but the words sat like peanut butter in her mouth.

Mama woke earlier than usual and came into Ruby's room.

"Get up, girl," Mama said. "We have somewhere to be."

"Where?" Ruby questioned, rubbing her eyes.

"We got a problem to solve," Mama said, like she was deciding on chicken or pork for dinner. Her mama was only thirty-seven now. She had birthed seven babies and was faced with the possibility of being a grandmother. In fact, the last baby boy just came in June.

Mama had never learned to drive a car, so she bundled up the baby and bought two bus tickets to West Plains.

The waiting room in the West Plains Women's Clinic smelled like alcohol, which immediately reminded Ruby of shot needles. Old Highlights magazines curled at the corners were stacked on a table. Ruby sat heart pounding like a drum too fast to follow. She was seventeen and pregnant, and the weight of it pressed into her ribs like a stone. She sat stiff in the chair beside Mama, her hands twisted in her lap. Her clothes were too tight, so she was wearing her chubby brother's red and blue striped shirt and jeans tied together with a rubber band.

"Mama, why are we here?" Ruby asked.

Mama didn't acknowledge her. She just tucked her pocketbook tighter under her arm. Her lips were pressed into a line that meant she wasn't in the mood for talking. She just bounced the baby on her shoulder, looking past the mess her daughter was in. When the nurse finally called them back, Ruby stood slow, like maybe if she didn't get up, none of this would be real.

Dr. McAfee was an older man with watery blue eyes and a voice that never lifted above a hush. He wore a white shirt with damp spots on the armpits and a green bow tie. His hair was crew cut style. He was low maintenance, and that was obvious. He didn't scold or judge, but he didn't smile either, just did the exam and then pulled his chair closer to mama, speaking low like Ruby wasn't even in the room.

"She's about six months along," he said. "Everything looks good. You can expect a baby the middle of January."

With that, he handed her a brochure that was titled, Everything You Need to Know About Having A Baby, by Dr. Benjamin Spock. Ruby wondered if Mama ever read anything by him. She doubted it seriously. If Dr. Spock had ever stepped foot in the Amsler house, he'd have set his book on fire and started over.

Ruby stared out the bus window all the way home. She felt like she was floating outside her body, watching it all from somewhere high above. She stared at the paper in her lap as the trees blurred past the window on the ride home. Everything you need to know—all crammed into ten pages. She figured that was about how much her mama had known, too. The road stretched out ahead, long and uncertain. She didn't know what she was going to do yet, but something inside her stirred—quiet, stubborn, and alive.

***

That night, Mama sent the boys out to hunt raccoons to make a stew. Said they had business to talk about with Ruby that didn't concern them. Ruby sat stoically in the worn, under-stuffed chair in the corner. Orville leaned in the door, and Mama sat on the vinyl couch.

Orville spoke up first, "We leaving next week for Gulfport, so you can have this child. We ain't even thinking about keeping it, 'cause you know you can't take care of no baby. It would cost me even more to feed another youngen, and since you ain't bringing in no extra money lately, we have to watch our spending more. You got yourself into a mess, girl and this is the only way out."

Mama chimed in," Orville said if you tried to keep it, they'd send you to jail."

"You think I wanted to be with those men?" Ruby's voice rose, sharp now, cutting through the stale air like broken glass. She stood up with her arms on her hips.

Mama interrupted, "You think folks are gonna believe you? A girl like you, already knocked up and sneaking around making trouble? They'll laugh you right outta that sheriff's office."

Standing up, Ruby screamed, "Maybe they'll lock him up for what he made me do!"

Orville turned slowly, "Watch your mouth, girl. You remember, I was the law in this town one time."

"I was only fifteen the first time you brought one of your friends around and told me to be sweet. Sixteen when you told me I owed it to the family to help where I could. You said it was just flirting, just company, that if I smiled nice and didn't complain, they'd pay so we could eat."

Orville's hand twitched at his side.

"You let them touch me and worse, "Ruby said, voice shaking but sure. "And when I cried, you said I should be grateful."

He stepped toward her, face gone red, jaw tight. "Girl, shut your damn—" his voice trailed off.

"I'm not a girl no more. You stole that girl!" Her whole body trembled. The truth had lived inside her like a sickness, twisting, eating, silencing. But now it spilled out—raw and sacred. "I didn't ask for this baby," she said. "But it is mine. And I'll die before I let you take it too."

Orville leaned over her, close enough she could smell the sour rot of coffee and fear on his breath. His voice dropped to a hiss. "You say that again to anyone, and I'll make you disappear. You and that bastard child. Don't think I won't."

A long silence. Then Orville straightened, shook his head like he was brushing dust off his shoulders, and walked out without another word.

Ruby looked at her mother through her tears and said, "It ain't fair."

Mama's eyes narrowed and responded. "Fair ain't never lived in this house."

Then, Mama stood up and smoothed her dress. "Ruby, one more thing. You better hide that shame so deep that God has to dig for it."

***

The next week, all six kids, Orville, and Mama were packed into that old rusty station wagon like Vienna Sausages, elbows jabbing and knees knocking. Mama held the baby in her arms beneath a mound of worn quilts. The heater hadn't worked in years, so they rode bundled in every coat they owned, breath fogging up the cracked windows, the cold creeping in through every rusted seam. Blankets got passed around like bread at supper, everybody trying to find a warm spot against someone else's shoulder. Orville didn't blink an eye or say a word while Mama and the older ones talked low and serious in the front, just kept his eyes on the road, hands gripping the wheel like he was holding onto more than just the car.

They arrived in Gulfport and pulled into the Hwy 90 Starlite Motel late at night. It felt like Ruby was being smuggled in the dark like something illegal. Her legs ached and her back felt like it was on fire. She needed to stretch out and pee. Mama ran out of peanut butter sandwiches when they stopped on the side of Hwy 49 to eat in Hattiesburg. Ruby's belly was empty and she wished she could just cross the road and go eat at that White Kitchen Chicken Diner.

Mom, Dad, and baby Earl took one bed, Ruby and Jimmy Dale slept in the other bed. The rest of the boys piled coats and blankets on the floor and fell right to sleep.

Ruby faced the window with metal slatted blinds, the sign of the restaurant blinking across the road. The red and white burn-out neon lights made the Indian look like he was in a war dance. Up and down and back again. Ruby imagined the Indian was chanting something about rain or war. She doubted they had a chant about fried chicken. Ruby slowly dozed off while thinking about food and how the hell she could save herself and this child from what was coming.

CHAPTER SEVENTEEN

THE BLONDE BABY

After thirteen hours of labor, a thin cry pierced the delivery room. Ruby strained to see her baby, but the bundle was carried away before she could touch her, before she could even breathe her in. All through the night, Ruby asked to hold her child, but the nurses passed by like she hadn't spoken, as if her words dissolved in the sterile air.

Then, as dawn softened the room, the door creaked open, and a metal bassinet rolled in. Ruby's heart slammed in her chest, and she leaned forward. A little card was clipped to the side.

> **DOB** – 1-6-62. 1:10 a.m.
>
> **Name:** Minnie.
>
> **Weight** 7 lbs, 8 oz. 19 inches.
>
> **Status:** 16 BFA—whatever that meant

Ruby's throat burned. Her name is not Minnie, she thought. She's not a number or a status.

The nurse said little, only lifted the swaddled bundle and placed her carefully into Ruby's arms.

"You can hold her for a little while," she murmured, "and say your goodbyes."

Then she slipped quietly from the room. Ruby looked at this baby wrapped in a blanket that was stamped with the name of the hospital.

The world seemed to stop. Ruby looked down at her baby girl—so impossibly perfect, with hair like spun gold catching the morning light. Not red, not brown, but shimmering soft as silk. She pressed her cheek against her daughter's and whispered, "Lora. Your name's Lora Elaine. I gave you that name 'fore I ever laid eyes on you. They might try an' change it, give you some fancy name that don't belong—but don't you forget, you're mine. Always gonna be mine." Ruby gave a shaky laugh, thinking about that Dr. Spock pamphlet. "Ain't no pamphlet in the world gonna tell me how to love you. Reckon he never wrote the chapter on lettin' go, anyhow."

Ruby kissed her tiny fingers, breathed in the sweet, new scent of her skin. She sang softly the old Indian song Papa Land had taught her—words she didn't understand but felt deep in her bones. She poured everything she had into that song, into the touch of her hand, into the way she memorized every dimple, every curve of her baby's face.

She leaned close, her voice barely more than breath. "Baby girl, you listen. You take the sweetness where it grows. Always pick the berries, don't let nobody tell ya you can't. And stand tall, strong as an oak on the ridge. Don't let the world break that spirit the Lord done give ya."

Ruby rocked her a little, letting the weight of the child settle against her chest. Her voice came low and thick, like the hills themselves were speaking through her.

"Lora, I can't keep ya now, but I swear to ya—Mama's gonna do better. I ain't stayin' the same anymore. I'll make somethin' of myself, I'll get strong, an' one day, I'll come back for you. You'll see me walk through that door, an' you'll know I kept my word. I'll be the mama you deserved right from the start." She pressed her lips to the baby's temple. "So, don't you give up on me, hear? You hold your head high, stand tall, be strong. And you remember, no matter where they take you—you're mine. You were mine first."

She hugged her baby to her chest, burying Lora's small face against her collarbone, eyes squeezed shut as if the world wouldn't exist if she didn't see it. The quiet weight of her daughter in her arms was the only thing that made the ache bearable—the rest of it, all the grief and fear she swallowed down, letting it live in the shadows where no one could witness it.

***

Ruby sat in the social worker's office, pen hovering over a stack of forms she didn't really want to fill out. Her eyes drifted to the walls—posters preaching the importance of polio shots, brochures scattered across the table showing radiant families with newborns. A framed print declared, "Family isn't built by genes; it's built by love." Ruby let out a bitter, quiet laugh. Love, she thought, shaking her head, wasn't building anything in her world—not for her, not ever.

A nice looking woman came to the door and welcomed her in. The room was hushed and glowing, the hum of the space heater wrapping the air in warmth. There were no windows, only one way in or out. Ruby wondered why anyone would build a room without a window, only darkness. She sat on the edge of the wheelchair, gown pulled tight at her knees, fingers trembling from the weight of love and loss mingled together.

Miss Fannie Wadlington waited a beat, then continued, "I'm a social worker at the Mississippi Children's Home in Jackson. I'm told that you are hesitant to place your baby for adoption."

Ruby looked at her with a stare reserved for her worst enemies and replied, "No, not hesitant, hell bound not to."

Miss Wadlington was not new to this game, and she didn't flinch. "You have not had an easy life, I know that. I don't need to know everything," she said. "But I know enough by watching the way you carry yourself." Ruby's throat tightened. The Social Worker leaned in, elbows on her knees. "What they did to you—whoever 'they' are—you didn't deserve it. And neither does she."

That made Ruby lift her eyes a little.

"You love your baby. I know that. I can feel it. But sometimes love isn't enough to keep a child safe from the world you grew up in. Sometimes the most loving thing you can do," she said carefully, "is break the cycle."

Tears welled up in Ruby's eyes and rolled down her freckled cheeks.

"You're still a just a girl, honey. And you were never given a chance to grow up safe." Miss Wadlington paused. "So, let me ask you this—if you keep her, and they come for her, the same way they came for you… what will you do then?"

Ruby's face crumpled. She could no longer keep it together. Her hands covered her mouth, her shoulders shaking with grief, fury, and guilt.

Mrs. Wadlington reached for her hand. "You can't go back and save yourself from what has happened to you, Ruby. But you can save her."

Silence. Ruby stared at the wall where a window should have been. She felt like she couldn't breathe in that tiny room. Then she whispered, barely audible, "She's the only thing that's ever been mine."

The social worker nodded, tears in her own eyes now.

"I know, Ruby. But she has her whole life ahead of her. And you have a chance to get out and do things differently." She cleared her throat and moved on. We have a family from the Delta, that's the northern part of the state, and they want a baby badly. The man has blue eyes and blonde hair, she favors him. He is deeply kind and patient. The woman is educated and a teacher. She dresses real nice and looks like Jane Wyman. They have their own home in the country and even have a horse. They have a nursery ready for her with baby butterflies and gingham curtains. She has a shelf full of toys and books already!"

She pictured the nursery—the butterflies, the curtains—but her mind wouldn't go there. It stayed on Lora's face.

"The grandparents are all so excited and wrote letters to us saying they all will welcome her and raise her up in the ways of the Lord."

Ruby didn't answer right away. Just turned her head toward the blank wall. After a long silence, she turned her face toward Mrs. Wadlington, and nodded just once.

***

Mama stood by the hospital window, arms folded tight, eyes fixed on the parking lot as if something better might pull in. Every so often, she adjusted her cat-eyeglasses, the gesture sharp and practiced—like she could straighten the whole world with just two fingers on a frame. Not once did she look at Ruby's face. Not once did she ask about the baby. The silence between them stretched long and sharp, like barbed wire. Her brother Jimmy Dale came with Mama. He climbed onto the chair beside her bed, legs swinging, and held Ruby's hand for a spell. He chattered the way only a little brother could, telling her how soon as Lora got bigger, they'd go play down by the river again, maybe chase armadillos through the brush. Ruby smiled weakly, but her heart felt so heavy it nearly split in two.

Ruby had gone through every sharp wave of labor alone, dropped at the hospital door like she was going to run an errand instead of bringing a child into the world. She wanted to reach out, to beg her mama to see her—not just the shame, not just the trouble, but her—but the words stuck like wool in her throat. All she could do was hold Jimmy Dale's small hand and listen to him giggle, wishing love could be that simple.

For the first time, Ruby found herself wondering about the demons her own mother was fighting. What storms had carved her so hard, made her so distant, so cold? She thought of the sharp lines in Mama's face, the way her eyes rarely softened, the quiet walls she kept between herself and the world. Ruby didn't understand it—not yet—but a small, aching part of her wanted to. She wanted to know what had shaped her mother into the woman who could stand so near and still feel so far. Maybe, she thought, love had never been gentle with her Mama either. Maybe it had been stripped away, one heartbreak at a time, until all that remained was a shell as tough as granite.

***

A week later, Ruby stood at the top of the hospital steps, coat too thin for the wind coming off the Gulf. Her body ached where it had been broken open, her heart felt worse. But her shoulders were square and her hands were steady. The door clicked behind her with a soft finality of something forever finished.

It was time to leave, to go back to the place where this all started. She didn't cry, now there was something new rising in her chest. The sky was gray, low, and bruised, but Ruby tilted her chin toward it anyway. People passed her on the sidewalk—nurses, bus drivers, old women with shopping bags—and no one looked twice. No one knew what she had left behind in that building. No one could see the hollow space where a baby had been.

But Ruby knew. She wasn't going back. Not to that house, not to her parents, not to the life she was given. She wouldn't just survive, she'd become someone Lora could be proud to find—if she ever came looking.

CHAPTER EIGHTEEN

AIN'T COMING BACK

The very next day, Ruby sat in the back seat of the station wagon, her cheek pressed to the cold glass of the window. It was the only thing that felt real—the baby was gone. Left behind at the hospital, tucked into a bassinet with a name card that just said Minnie.

In the front seat, Jimmy Dale twisted around, voice small. "Mama... where's Ruby's baby?"

Their mama kept her eyes on the road and her hands tight on the wheel. After what seemed like hours, Mama said, "She cost too much money and we ain't got no room for a baby in this car. That's all there is to it."

Jack, Ruby's next-to-last brother, turned toward Ruby, his freckled face peering over the seat. "Was she real sweet?"

Jimmy Dale spoke up in that curious way little boys did when they ain't quite figured out when to leave things alone.

"But I wanted to hold her, I woulda held her all the way home!"

"What color was her hair, Ruby?" Jack inquired.

"Blonde," Ruby said quietly.

"Blonde!" Jimmy Dale inserted excitedly.

Aunt Lena said, "Blonde babies are unusual in the hills." Ruby thought back to Aunt Lena's words. "Blonde babies," she'd say, rocking back on her heels and lowering her voice like she was letting Ruby in on a secret, "they got a kinda magic most folks don't notice. They can see things before they happen, hear the wind talk, an feel the hearts of folks 'round 'em. Lord knows, they got a way of changin' a room, settin' folks at ease, makin' trouble slip right past 'em sometimes."

Mama interrupted Ruby's thoughts when she yelled, "She's staying at the hospital. That's all y'all need to know. Those folks'll take care of her proper. We ain't discussin' it no more!"

Ruby froze, the words pressing down on her chest, stealing the air from her lungs. Her thoughts, already scattered, fell silent under Mama's sharp edge. She looked at the back of Orville's head in the seat in front of her. He was leaned back, smoking and listening to George Jones, but he didn't make a sound. His eyes stayed fixed on the blur of pine trees along Highway 49, seeing but not seeing, letting the road roll past like it belonged to someone else. He carried a calm, practiced distance, as if none of it—the hospital, the baby, the heartbreak—had anything to do with him. In his mind, he could press a switch and make it all vanish, forget it ever happened. He had a way of making his sins disappear as if they'd never existed—no guilt, no remorse, no flicker of conscience to betray him. Everything he'd done, every wrong choice, every cut he'd left in other people's lives, he could just leave behind, untouchable and unfeeling. Orville didn't have to follow the rules of heaven or earth. He went by his own book, Ruby thought, written by the devil himself. She couldn't help but wonder what that book was called, but she was sure her father had somehow read it cover to cover.

Later, as the station wagon roared toward the rolling hills of the Ozarks, Ruby felt a hollow tug in her chest. The familiar ridges and hollers stretched past her window, but she knew deep down it wouldn't be home—not really. Home wasn't a place you returned to; it was where your heart could rest, where the people you loved were safe. And her heart was with Lora. Wherever she was, that was where Ruby belonged. No ridge, no hollow, no town in the Ozarks could claim her—not when the tiny, golden-haired girl she had just held in her arms was out there in the world.

Ruby laid her head back on the seat and closed her eyes. Behind her eyelids, all she could see was a blanket stamped with a faded logo: Property of Gulfport Memorial Hospital.

***

February came around, and the sky went soft with a peach-colored hush as the sun dipped low behind the ridge. Supper was done, dishes clattered in the kitchen, and the porch creaked under Orville's boots as he sat, smoking in silence.

Ruby stepped outside, not meaning to say a word. She just needed air and to look at the stars.

Orville sat on the porch but didn't look at her. Just took a drag and stared out across the pasture, where the fireflies were starting to come out.

After a long, quiet minute, he said without turning, "She'd be 'bout two months now, would she?" Ruby stopped mid-step. Her breath caught. That was the first time he'd said anything. Not in Mississippi. Not on the drive home. Not in the months since.

"Yeah" Ruby said, barely above a whisper. Silence stretched out between them, brittle and long.

The porch creaked again as Orville shifted in his chair. Ruby didn't mean to look at him, but something drew her eyes up. The way his mouth pulled tight. The way his jaw clenched like he was holding something back.

And for just a second—just a flicker in the dying light—Ruby thought she saw it. A tear glinting in the corner of his eye.

But that was impossible. Orville didn't cry. He was made of hickory and flint and old tobacco spit. He didn't have tears.

So, Ruby looked away, pretending she hadn't seen. She stepped off the porch and into the yard and picked up a shirt one of the boys left in the dirt. The fireflies blinked like stars.

But for just one moment, she let herself believe Orville might care too. Just a little. Even if neither of them would ever speak it plain.

Ruby stood straight. "I'm goin' to Patsy's. I start at the cannery Monday."

Patsy Doyle was Ruby's friend, a girl she had met last fall, who had just moved to Norwood a few months earlier. She was a little older than Ruby but still lived in the house with her mama and stepfather. Patsy was a fiery brunette, with the kind of striking looks that reminded Ruby of Ava Gardner—if Ava Gardner hadn't had the money. She always wore bright red lipstick and carried a devilish smile that hinted at trouble and mischief, fearless in a way that made everyone around her take notice. Standing at least five-eleven and graceful as a swan, Patsy towered over Ruby, who still had a girlish figure, short and petite, making Patsy's presence all the more commanding. She had graduated from high school and was sharp as a tack, quick to learn and quicker to notice things others missed. Patsy protected Ruby fiercely and knew all of Ruby's secrets—well, most of them—and never judged, never let anyone else touch them. She kept up with all the Hollywood gossip, reading every scandal and starlet's fall from grace, devouring true crime stories with the same appetite, fascinated by the dark twists of human nature. She worked in the office at the cannery and walked around like she owned the place, commanding attention and respect with every step. A notorious flirt, she rarely gave men more than a passing glance; she was searching for a certain kind of man—someone who had seen the world, could match her wit, and carried just enough danger to keep her heart racing, someone she couldn't ignore even if she tried. He certainly wasn't to be found in Christian County.

Orville just laughed, "A job? You'll come runnin' back soon enough. You have it good, girl, and you don't appreciate nothin'."

"I won't be back," she said, quiet and final.

Orville's face twisted, but something in her voice—something he hadn't heard before—made him stop short. All he could do was step off the porch and walk out to the shed.

Ruby didn't wait. She had already gathered her things in a brown paper sack, making sure she didn't leave her dream journal or the locket Clyde had given her. She carried her things to the end of the gravel, where Patsy waited in her old car, the engine knocking like a heart too tired to keep beat. Ruby opened the back door, put her belongings on the seat, opened the front door, and climbed in. Patsy didn't say a word, just put it in gear and drove away.

***

Life at the Doyles' was completely different from anything Ruby had ever known. Patsy's mama, Wila Jean, was a quiet woman with a permanent, gentle smile. Ruby had never heard her speak a bad word about anyone. Every evening, Wila Jean would ask about their day at work, and they would sit together at a real table, sharing a simple meal. No one hit, no one cursed, and no one told Ruby she was worthless. In fact, Wila Jean complimented her constantly, telling her how much she appreciated Ruby helping out around the house—trivial things that Ruby didn't quite know how to feel about.

The Doyles even had a washing machine, so Ruby's hands finally started to heal—no more scrubbing by hand, just hanging the clothes to dry. They had an indoor bathroom, a luxury she had never known, and she and Patsy shared a cozy bedroom with a chest of drawers and a closet. A real double bed off the ground with a genuine mattress. Ruby had never been in a place so fancy, and even the smallest details—a porch that didn't sag, flowers and grass in the lawn, the smooth floors, the warm water, the quiet hum of the washer—made her feel like she had stepped into a different world.

Patsy's stepfather, Howard, had his own kind of charm. He would grin and say, "Ruby, you bashful as a butterfly on a broom handle,"

Ruby would try not to blush.

She was used to paying for her keep—she'd been doing it for years—so it came naturally that she offered to pay the Doyles for her stay. After her first two weeks, she came into the kitchen where Wila Jean was folding towels and handed her five dollars, a small token of gratitude for the kindness that already felt like home.

"Girl, what's this for?" Wila Jean asked, looking down at Ruby's hand.

"It's my rent," Ruby said, "On account I gotta pay my way."

Mrs. Doyle blinked, genuinely shocked. "Ruby, we didn't ask you to stay here 'cause we need help with the rent. We need to help you."

Ruby heard the words, but they didn't land quite right.

"I ain't lookin' for no handout," she said. "I can pull my own weight. You been mighty kind to me, and I appreciate it so much."

Wila Jean tilted her head a little, soft smile spreading across her face. She reached for Ruby's hand, not rushing, letting the moment linger.

With a voice as warm and sweet as biscuits and honey, she said, "Ruby, we all need a soft place to land sometimes."

And with that, she gently opened Ruby's fingers and placed the worn money back into her hand, letting Ruby feel the weight of kindness she had rarely known before.

***

Each morning, Ruby pulled her hair back with a rubber band, slipped on her Neosho Cannery uniform, and climbed in the car with Patsy. She was happy to give Ruby a ride each day, and Ruby would put gas in her car for the trouble. The work was hard and loud—her fingers burned from the tomato acid and her back ached from hours on her feet—but every Friday, she cashed her paycheck and tucked nearly every dollar into a coffee can beneath her bed.

She was saving—every penny she could scrounge. For bus fare. For a room. For a lawyer, maybe. For anything that could help her find Lora. Her arms were stronger now, her face thinner and more defined. And her heart—oh, her heart—held a kind of fire that hadn't been there before. Every night, she'd whisper her baby's name, her lips brushing the quiet air, and say, "Mama's comin'. I don't know how long, but I'm comin.'"

It was the only promise she had ever made that truly mattered. And this time, nobody—not Orville, not poverty, not fear—was going to stop her.

CHAPTER NINETEEN

SAM LINK

Ruby met Martha Link when she went to work at the cannery. Martha was bubbly and spirited, with curly blonde hair that bounced around her shoulders and silver-rimmed glasses that slipped down her nose when she laughed. She was two years older than Ruby. Her sweet face, round and rosy-cheeked like a cherub, seemed to glow with an easy cheerfulness. She was always chattering about what she'd heard on the radio, what she'd read in those glossy glamour magazines, or—most of all—her boyfriend Jim, who was stationed in Vietnam with the Air Force.

"He's comin' back on leave soon!" she'd gush, eyes sparkling. "And we've got all these plans—picnics, dances, maybe a drive down to Eureka Springs if we can swing it!"

Ruby mostly just listened, smiling faintly, feeling a quiet distance between them, as if Martha's bright, hopeful world belonged somewhere else entirely.

On Tuesday, Martha asked, "Hey, Ruby, wanna come for dinner Friday night? Mama's cookin' up a big meal, and all my brothers and sisters are comin'."

That said a lot—Martha was one of eight, maybe nine kids. With spouses and grandkids, it would be a whole crowd, a real hullabaloo of folks. Ruby hesitated, but the thought of something different—something beyond the monotony—lifted her heart.

"Sure," she said. "That sounds nice... if you're sure there's room for me."

Martha laughed, the sound like little bells. "Course there is! Mama makes room for everybody. I'll send someone by to fetch you 'round six."

Ruby nodded, feeling a little flutter in her belly she didn't recognize.

When Friday came, Ruby got home and dressed in something that didn't smell like tomato sauce, brushed her hair down, and pinned a little butterfly clip to the side. She looked in the mirror and saw someone a little older, a little wiser—not quite a woman but not the girl who had been through so much, either. Just... Ruby, standing somewhere in between, feeling different for the first time.

She waited on the porch, heart skipping a little, until the headlights rounded the curve and the car came to a stop. A tall, lean figure stepped out. In a gentle voice he asked, "You Ruby?"

She nodded, a shy little smile tugging at her lips.

"Well, come on, girl," he said. "I'm Sam."

***

The screen door slammed behind the last sister just as Mr. Link said, "Amen." Nobody had to say it was time to eat, they had lots of practice in being sure to get a piece of chicken and a biscuit with this crowd. Ruby looked around the room and down the table. Martha had insisted she sit at the main dining table with the adults. Ruby had stopped counting at thirty-two bodies, seated at card tables and on the sofa and on the floor. All ages, shapes, and sizes. All belonging in some way to each other.

Martha's Mom had cast iron pots of green beans with potatoes, wilted salad in bacon grease, creamed corn, macaroni with piping hot cheese, homemade pickles and cucumber, sliced tomatoes, butterbeans, a big, sliced ham, biscuits, and a huge pan of cornbread. On the desert table sat a rhubarb cobbler as fine as Ruby had ever seen. The men gathered on one end talkin' about rain, no rain, hay, and tractors. The women sat near Ruby and discussed babies, who was pregnant and who ran off with who from the Gospel Tabernacle church. Ruby sat stoic and amazed at all the happy chatter. Not a one of them had cussed, thrown mashed potatoes, or knocked anybody out of the chair. They were like real, civilized people, and Ruby was unfamiliar with just how to be in that. She felt small—not the kind from being young but from not fitting in.

Somebody told a story about the old lady at church with her dress stuck in her girdle, and Ruby couldn't stop herself. She roared with laughter like she didn't remember ever doing before.

Someone said, "Well, there she is."

Ruby wasn't used to hearing jokes from people that weren't about her. She turned beet red from embarrassment just as she caught Sam's eye. But she didn't look away. They both just smiled and went back to eating their dinner.

***

Ruby didn't see Sam for a week. But she thought about him—more than she meant to. That tall, still figure with the long face, black-rimmed glasses, and the careful way he moved. No swagger, no sideways grin. A real man who didn't waste a word and didn't flinch when she looked tired or worn thin.

The second time she saw him was at the feed store. He was carrying a sack of cracked corn for an older man, glasses slipping down his nose, sweat darkening the back of his shirt. He looked up, saw her, and gave her the smallest nod. Not a smile. Just acknowledgment. Like he'd been expecting her. Like she belonged in the same frame of his quiet life.

After that, it was once every week or two—around town, passing by Patsy's house, or riding around the square. Sam never pressed. Just asked how she was doing.

One evening, Patsy and Ruby were sitting in the yard, watching the fireflies flicker like tiny lanterns and talking about a murder—some doctor in Mississippi that Patsy had read about in True Detective magazine. Patsy's voice was low and conspiratorial, full of the thrill she got from reading about crimes far away, while Ruby shivered a little in the warm night air, half fascinated, half uneasy. "You know," Patsy said, "his girlfriend did it. She was jealous of the wife and she let him have it! Look at her in this photo, she looks like she doesn't even care!"

Ruby just had a brief thought that she was happy Lora's new daddy wasn't a doctor.

Then they heard the rumble of a Bel Air rolling up the driveway, its tires crunching on the gravel. Sam got out and walked over to the girls.

Patsy, ever the tease, let out a provocative little hum, something like, "Well, hello there..."

Sam just smiled, but his eyes didn't leave Ruby. There was a quiet intensity about him that made her heart skip a beat.

"Ruby," he said plainly, his voice steady, "I want to take you out. A real date. Not just a walk or a milkshake—something proper. You and me."

Ruby felt a little flutter in her chest. The words were simple, but the way he said them made them feel like the first promise of something she hadn't known she'd been waiting for.

Ruby's heart skipped, then dropped. She hesitated, swallowing the lump in her throat. *He can't be talking to me*, she thought. *What could he possibly need from me?*

"I—I'm busy," she stammered, stepping back. "Ain't got time for that right now."

Patsy chimed in, "You ain't got nothin' to do— you got all the time in the world."

Ruby gave her a look that said, "Wait till he leaves, you're done for!"

Sam's brow furrowed, but he didn't push. Just nodded, quiet. "Okay then. If you change your mind..." Then he climbed back into the car and drove away.

Later that evening, Ruby sat on the bed with Patsy, her closest friend and a voice of fire in her life.

"You're scared, ain't you?" Patsy said softly but firm. "You just about a dumb ass, Ruby. He is as fine a guy as they make in these hollers."

Ruby nodded, eyes down. "I don't know how to be something he would be proud to have on his arm."

"Then you gotta learn," Patsy said, voice rising like the wind before a storm. "You got one life, Ruby. Ain't no use wasting it on bein' scared. You want change, you gotta have the courage to step into it and wear the red lipstick."

Ruby laughed at the lipstick, 'cause Patsy always wore it, with her beautiful black hair. Even Ruby knew redheads didn't wear red lipstick, and she didn't own a piece of makeup.

Patsy stood and rummaged through her closet. "I got the perfect dress for you. Real pretty—like you deserve. Saturday afternoon. I'll dress you up special, show you how to be the woman you wanna be."

Ruby hesitated a moment, then nodded. "Alright."

That afternoon, just after work, Patsy drove Ruby to the Conoco station. Ruby's heart fluttered with a mix of nerves and excitement—today, she was finally going to tell Sam that she would take the date. The car rumbled along the road, and every turn brought her a little closer to the moment she'd been thinking about all week.

Sam was talking to the old men playing checkers. He walked over to the car and leaned in, looking at Ruby straight in the eyes, "Ladies, how are you all this evenin'?"

Ruby took a big swallow, and before she could change her mind, she said, "I'll take that date this weekend. If the offer is still good."

Sam smiled and hit his hand on the door. "I'll see you at six."

***

Saturday was a flurry of excitement. Ruby had never been on a real date, and she couldn't believe it was happening. It was hard to believe that a real good man like Sam would want to spend time with her. He had been in the service, the end of Korea, and had seen a lot of the world.

She sat on the bed while Patsy pulled an A-line dress from the closet that was unlike anything Ruby had ever worn. It was a soft, sky-blue lace that caught the light like a whisper of the summer sky, delicate and full of quiet promise. The lace was sheer and floral, layered over a smooth, light cotton lining that brushed gently against the skin.

Down the front, a neat row of small gold buttons glinted like drops of sunshine, each one polished just enough to catch the eye without being showy. The dress fit perfectly—nipped in at the waist to trace the shape Ruby was still learning to recognize, with sleeves that ended just past the elbow in a gentle flare, soft and graceful.

It wasn't flashy or loud. It was hope stitched into fabric—a promise of something new and beautiful waiting just around the bend. Patsy said it was perfect for a real date, she said she saw Natalie Wood wear one just like it a few months back in the Ladies Home Journal. And as Ruby held it up, she felt a little spark of courage flicker inside her, as if the dress might help her find the woman she was ready to become.

Patsy took Ruby by the hand and led her into her small kitchen, where the old radio played soft country tunes and sunlight spilled through the lace curtains. On the worn wooden table lay a pair of sharp scissors, a comb, and a bright blue ribbon.

"Time to lose that Pentecostal ponytail," Patsy said with a grin, tugging Ruby's thick hair away from her face.

Ruby watched, heart pounding, as Patsy carefully snipped away the ragged ends, letting fall the weight of years of worry and weariness to the floor in soft red curls. She worked with practiced hands, cutting and teasing, shaping the hair into something lighter, something freer.

When Patsy was done, Ruby barely recognized herself in the mirror. Her hair was shorter now—soft waves that framed her face and lifted her eyes. Patsy added a few playful curls at the ends.

"We don't need the bow," Patsy determined, "you look just right like this."

Patsy stepped back, admiring her work, "Fresh start. You look like you just might want to smile for real."

CHAPTER TWENTY

THE BEL-AIR AND THE BIG WORLD

Sam pulled into the gravel drive right on time, his 1958 Bel Air gleaming like something off a magazine cover. It was shiny yellow, with chrome that caught the last of the day's light and a black interior smooth as butter. The tires were clean, the windows down, and the whole thing hummed low and smooth like it knew it didn't belong on a dirt road.

Ruby stepped out onto the porch in her blue lace dress, the gold buttons catching the sunset, her curls bouncing soft around her shoulders. For a second, she didn't move. Sam stepped out, tall and neat in a white shirt, black slacks, and a plaid jacket. "Evenin'," he said, opening the passenger door with one hand like it was the most natural thing in the world. "You look... well, better than Springfield deserves."

Ruby laughed nervously and ducked her head. "Where we goin'?"

He looked sideways at her with a grin. "Napolitano's."

She blinked. "Napa—what?"

He laughed a little and repeated, "Napolitano's," Like it should mean something to Ruby.

She shook her head, brow furrowed. "Is that... is that a restaurant?"

"Sure is," he chuckled. He adjusted his glasses. "Up in Springfield."

Ruby's eyes widened. "Springfield?"

Sam nodded, calm and steady. "Thought we'd do somethin' a little special."

Ruby's stomach flipped. That felt like a world away. Her family only ever went up there for supplies, hospital visits, or court. They never ate out, never dressed up, never did things like this. A fancy restaurant? Not only didn't she know what fork to use, she didn't even know there was more than one kind. She hoped they spoke English.

Sam reached out and gently touched her hand where it rested on her skirt.

"You're allowed to have a good night, Ruby. You earned it. Just ride with me. Nothin' to be nervous about."

Then he smiled, slow and kind, with a twinkle in his eye that made her chest loosen just a bit.

Without another word, he turned the key, and the radio came to life—Dion's "Runaround Sue" burst through the dash, bright and bold. Sam reached over and turned it up, then bobbed his head along with the beat like it was the best sound he'd heard all day.

Ruby couldn't help it—she laughed. A real laugh, full in her chest.

As the final notes of the song faded into the low hum of the radio, Sam pulled back just slightly, enough to look at her.

"You know somethin'?" he said, voice quiet as dusk. "That dress suits you."

Ruby looked down, a little bashful.

"Patsy made me wear it," she murmured. "Said I needed to look like someone who had a reason to smile."

Sam gave a small nod, his gaze steady on her face. "It ain't just the dress," he said, tilting his head. "It's your eyes."

Ruby blinked, caught off guard.

"They're the same shade," he went on. "That soft kind of blue—not loud but... deep. Like a sky just before the storm lets up. I used to have an old bird dog with eyes that same color, ol' Jake, he was somethin'. He could pick up a trail clean and quiet, work that field like a champion." His voice trailed off.

Ruby wasn't sure whether to be offended or in love, but either way, she was smitten.

"Hey, listen to me run my mouth like a creek," Sam said. "Sorry—I get to talkin' about dogs and forget what special company I'm in."

She looked away, cheeks warm, not used to hearing words like that about herself.

Sam grinned, that familiar twinkle lighting up his eyes. "Blue Eyes," he said, like he was trying the name out on his tongue. "I think that's what I'll call you."

Ruby laughed, just a little. "You givin' me a dog nickname now?

"Seems right fittin'," he said, his smile easy and sure. Blue Eyes suits you better than Ruby anyway. You've got too much softness for a name that sharp."

She shook her head, but she was smiling—really smiling, like her heart was light enough to float. Alright then," she said, voice barely above a whisper. "Blue Eyes it is."

Napolitano's was a real, authentic Italian place on Walnut Street. It was so dark inside, Ruby's eyes had to adjust. The tables were covered in red and white checked cloths covering heavy wooden tables and a candle wrapped in mesh flickering in the centers. It reminded her of True Crime Magazine's write up of the Al Capone Gang. It sure felt like Al would fit right in here. Mr. Tony, the owner, even came by and asked how their food was and made a comment about how lucky Sam was to have such a pretty date. Ruby was relieved when he spoke to her in a language she could understand.

In the corner, a man who looked close to ninety played the organ, occasionally switching over to the piano. Every so often, he'd announce his name, reminding the crowd that he was Henry. A clear jar on the piano, marked in red, said: TIPS APPRECIATED. Most of the music he played was the kind Grandmother Land would have liked, but every now and then, he slipped in a Nat King Cole tune or an Elvis number. Sometimes he played so loudly that Ruby couldn't hear what Sam was saying, and she didn't want to miss a single word. Henry seemed to pour his life into the music, as he played every note from heart. It was a good thing he didn't need to see the notes, those dark sunglasses he wore surely wouldn't allow that. Ruby suddenly wondered if he was completely blind.

In between songs, an unseen beat continued, a soft cha... cha... cha... that seemed to pulse through the room, weaving itself into the fading notes and keeping the rhythm alive long after Henry's fingers left the keys.

Ruby had no idea what to order for dinner, so Sam ordered for them both. So many dishes that she hadn't ever eaten, other than spaghetti. The Doyle's cooked that every other Tuesday night.

Sam had spent a little time in Italy on his way to Pork Chop Hill in the war.

They had just finished the last bites of manicotti and lasagna when a server came by with a tiny dustpan and broom and whisked away their crumbs. Ruby's eyes widened, and she started to giggle. She was afraid she wouldn't stop, scattered with crumbs and the faint scent of garlic still lingering in the air, when Sam stood up from the booth. Ruby thought he was headed to the restroom, but instead, he walked over to Henry and whispered something to him and slipped something into the tip jar.

Moments later, the room shifted, hushed by the slow, familiar croon of

Elvis Presley drifting from the speakers. It was the kind of song that didn't just play—it settled deep into your bones, all tender ache and impossible longing.

Sam returned to the table and held out his hand. Ruby froze. She knew how to stomp through a cotton-eyed joe, but this—this was different. Slow, close, terrifying.

Then, as if from nowhere, she heard Grandpa Land's voice steady in her head. "Courage ain't about killin' the bear, Ruby girl—it's about learnin' to live with it."

She took a breath, pushed herself up, and let Sam lead her onto the floor. They were the only ones out there, the crowd fading into shadow. He guided her arms around his neck and set his hands gently at her waist.

Bending low, his breath warm against her ear, Sam teased, "You follow directions better than old Jake."

Ruby burst into nervous laughter, the knot in her chest loosening. The music curled around them like a promise, and for the first time, she let herself sink into it—into him—into the possibility of being carried by something she didn't have to fight.

CHAPTER TWENTY-ONE

A WAY TO LIVE DECENT

Sam's family had taken to Ruby right away. The Links were loud and full of laughter, the kind of people who never ran out of stories or fried chicken. Ruby felt at home there in a way she rarely had before. They made work seem like play—hauling hay, milking cows, teasing one another between chores.

One morning, Sam had talked her into driving the tractor. He told her where the gears were but forgot to mention the brake. She took off too fast, and before she knew it, she'd plowed right through a section of fence. The boys hollered, Sam doubled over laughing, and Ruby jumped down red-faced and hollering right back at him.

"You could've warned me!" she shouted, but even she couldn't stop laughing once she saw Sam's grin.

Later, he told her, "You'll get it next time. You just need a little more practice."

She rolled her eyes. "Or a better teacher."

Those days were full of small joys—milk on her hands, hay in her hair, laughter echoing across the barnyard. Ruby loved the feeling of freedom and safety, laughing without worry, her heart light in a way it hadn't been in years.

"You know," Mrs. Link said one morning as they sipped coffee on the porch, "we were worried about Sam when he came back from the war. He seemed... different. Quiet. But ever since he met you, Ruby, he's a lot happier. You've done him good."

Ruby felt a flush in her cheeks, both pleased and shy. She caught Sam's eye across the porch and saw him smile softly, the kind of quiet, real smile that made her chest ache with warmth.

But there was one thing Ruby dreaded—Sam wanted to meet her folks.

"I don't know why you'd want to," she said one afternoon as they sat by the creek. "They ain't exactly friendly."

"Because they're your folks," Sam said simply. "If I'm gonna marry you someday, I better meet the people who made you."

"That's what worries me," Ruby picked at a dandelion stem. "You might change your mind."

He just smiled. "I already know enough to keep it made up."

When the day came, Ruby's stomach twisted the whole drive. Her hands wouldn't stop fidgeting. Sam kept telling her it'd be fine, but she wasn't convinced.

They pulled up to the house, the screen door creaking as Millie stepped out, arms folded, eyes sharp as ever. Orville was sitting on the porch, cleaning his shotgun, the barrel catching the sunlight. Ruby's heart skipped a beat—she was sure he was sending a silent warning—but Sam didn't flinch. Orville didn't intimidate him in the least.

"Well," Orville said, looking Sam over, "You sure you know what you're doin', boy?"

Sam smiled easily. "Reckon I do, sir."

Orville blinked, caught off guard, then gave a short laugh.

Millie just sipped her coffee and didn't have a thing to say.

On Saturdays, Sam sometimes took her into town just for fun. He bought her a cherry Coke and a bag of popcorn when they ducked into the Ritz Theatre to see To Kill a Mockingbird. Ruby sat with her hands folded tight, eyes fixed on the screen, feeling something stir in her she couldn't name.

Afterward, they strolled down Main Street, sharing sips of soda, laughing at silly things Sam had to say. She loved the small details—the tinkling bell of the pharmacy door, the smell of fresh bread from the bakery, the feel of Sam's arm brushing hers as they walked.

As they passed the courthouse, Sam asked, "When you were little, did you ever come to town just for fun? Not for errands or work—just because you wanted to?"

Ruby shook her head. "No. Mama didn't see much use in foolin' around."

She stopped by the courthouse steps and thought back to the day she'd gotten into that fight—the sting of spilled popcorn, the shouts, the way her heart had hammered in her chest. How long ago that seemed.

She gave a little laugh. "Funny," she said softly, "how different things can get."

Sam squeezed her hand. "Funny how much better they can get, too."

Later that night, after things quieted down, Ruby and Sam sat outside on the porch swing outside the Doyle's home.

Ruby looked over at him and said, "You never talk much about the war, Sam. Was it real bad?"

He was quiet for a long moment, eyes fixed on the dark beyond the yard.

"You see things over there that don't fit right in your head after," he said finally. "You come home, and the world's still spinning like nothin' ever happened, but you ain't the same. You try to act like you are, but you ain't."

Ruby swallowed, feeling the ache behind his words. "You ever wish you could forget it?" she asked softly.

Sam shook his head. "Forgetting don't fix nothin'. If you forget, you're bound to let it all happen again. Best you can do is remember and still find a way to live decent."

Ruby watched him in the dark, noticing the steady way he held himself, the calm certainty in his hands, even as his eyes carried old shadows. She realized then that Sam had a kind of quiet strength she hadn't seen in anyone else—a man who could carry his past without letting it crush the people he loved. And in that moment, she felt a flicker of hope she hadn't dared to name before. Maybe, just maybe, she could trust that he'd stand by her. That thought settled in her chest like sunlight through the barn loft—warm, steady, and impossible to ignore.

He reached over and took her hand, his thumb brushing across her knuckles.

"That's what I'm trying to do, Ruby," he said. "Find a way to live decent."

She didn't say anything back, just leaned against him, listening to the rhythm of the swing and the sound of his heart steady beside hers. And she didn't say it out loud, but deep down, she knew—this was the beginning of her real life.

***

The Maitland Music Fest was a big deal in the Ozarks, and it would be packed with people. The annual festival was always held the second Saturday of October. Ruby wore her best skirt, a white cotton blouse, and a blue scarf around her neck. Sam laced his fingers through hers as they walked through the festival gates. For once, no one stared. No whispered sideways glances, no snide looks tucked behind church-lady smiles. Just music and sun and the sweet, easy feeling of belonging.

Sam was proud—she could feel it in the way he held her hand a little tighter, in the smile that didn't leave his face all afternoon. He introduced her to every friend they passed, calling her "my girl" with an ease that made her heart bloom. A photographer was roaming around taking pictures and asked if they wanted theirs taken. Sam immediately responded," We sure do!" So, they perched on the bale of hay and smiled. The flash was so bright it nearly blinded Ruby. Sam laughed and danced around her like they were the only ones there.

The festival smelled like fried dough and cut grass and the thick sweetness of roasted corn. There were ribs on the smoker, glistening and caramelized, and someone was squeezing lemons into giant jugs of sugar water, ice clinking against glass as the line snaked around the stand. Ruby and Sam shared a funnel cake, warm and powdered with sugar so fine it dusted her nose, and he kissed it off with a grin.

Somewhere near the bandstand, a fiddle warbled into a bluegrass tune that got into your feet whether you meant to dance or not. Children danced and folks clapped in time, and the whole world felt stitched together with song. Ruby leaned against Sam's chest as the sun began to dip, the sky softening to sherbet colors, and she could feel the beat of his heart in time with the drums.

It was the kind of day she'd hold onto. One where she wasn't someone to be fixed or forgiven. She was just herself—laughing, full-bellied, hands sticky with lemonade and sugar, and wrapped in the warm safety of Sam's arm.

As the last chords of the final song drifted out into the night air, people began folding chairs and saying long goodbyes. Sam squeezed her hand and looked down at her with a quiet smile.

"Ready to head out?"

Ruby nodded, not because she wanted to leave but because even the leaving was sweet when you were walking away with someone who wanted you exactly as you were.

They rode in silence for a long stretch after Ruby's voice faded into the hum of the tires and the low murmur of the radio. The road twisted through the hollers, moonlight slipping in through the windshield, casting silver on her hands where they lay clenched in her lap.

She didn't look at him—couldn't. Her heart was beating like a trapped bird, her thoughts tumbling faster than she could catch them. Would he ever ask about her past? Would he want to know everything? Would he see her different, would he hate her?

Finally, Sam spoke. His voice was so calm, so sure, it caught her off guard.

"I been thinkin', maybe we should get married."

Ruby was stunned. She couldn't look at him, she took a deep breath and said, "Sam, there are some things I need to tell you 'bout. It may change your mind."

Sam eased the Chevy onto the shoulder, the headlights throwing a pale tunnel of light against the trees. Dust lifted and hung in the beams, then slowly drifted away. He slid the gear into park and let the engine idle low, the sound filling the quiet. For a second, he just sat there, his hand loose on the wheel, his other arm resting along the back of the seat. Then he turned toward her, his face half-shadowed by the dash glow, steady but carrying something heavy. Ruby's hands were tight in her lap, her eyes fixed forward until she felt the weight of his gaze. He let out a breath, slow and measured, like he'd been holding it a long while. "Ruby," he said, his voice low but steady, "You don't need to tell me nothin' you're scared of sayin'. I already know the only things that matter. You. Me. And the future we could have if we're brave enough to take it."

He paused, fingers drumming the wheel once before he stilled them. "There's a job comin' open in Lincoln—big project, buildin' a mall. My uncle Jeb's on it, and he promised me a place. Good pay. Schools better than what's here. We could get out, start fresh."

Then he turned fully to her, eyes glinting in the dim glow. "And we need that school—for Lora." Sam kept his eyes on her, steady as a stone. His voice was low, but there wasn't a tremble in it.

Ruby had no idea how to respond. Her mouth parted like she might say something, but nothing came. The words tangled in her throat, too heavy to push out. She stared out the windshield, heart pounding so hard she swore Sam could hear it. She wanted to say yes. She wanted to throw her arms around him, to believe every promise he was laying down. But fear clamped her still. What if it all slipped away the moment she reached for it.

"How did you know about her?"

"I didn't hear until later... and it killed me knowing you had to handle it all on your own," he replied. "Ruby, listen to me. We ain't waitin' around for life to happen anymore. April's just a few months off. We'll get married, and then we'll go straight to Mississippi. We'll find Lora together."

He reached across the seat, his rough hand covering hers.

"She deserves her mama back. And you—" his jaw tightened just a little, "you deserve to have her in your arms again. We'll make a home where she don't ever have to wonder if she's wanted."

He gave the faintest smile then, almost boyish. "Say yes, Ruby. Let's go get her."

CHAPTER TWENTY-TWO

J.C. PENNEY

They planned a small wedding at his family church near Sparta, on March 16th. Just family. That still meant a bunch of people, since they both had huge families. Of course, she included the Doyle's although they weren't officially related. She really didn't want to have her parents there at all, but Sam convinced her it was the right thing. Ruby believed what Sam said, and she knew he would keep her safe from smart comments that Orville might hurl her way. Sam's family planned a small reception in the hall of the church. His mama was making a white wedding cake with yellow roses, and his sister Cathy was bringing her famous pineapple and 7-Up punch.

The next few weeks were a blur. Ruby and Patsy drove to Springfield to pick out a dress to wear. Ruby carefully took ten dollars of the runaway money she had been saving to splurge on something special to wear. As they pulled into the parking lot of J. C. Penney, they headed straight to the dress department.

Patsy told Ruby, "If you come out with anything with polka dots and shoulder pads, I'm leavin' you here!" Ruby slung back her head and laughed a little too loud.

She browsed the racks of ready-to-wear and church dresses, holding each one up and trying to picture herself in it.

Suddenly, a saleslady appeared from around the corner and asked politely, "What are you looking for today?" Ruby's voice was soft as she replied, "A dress… for a wedding."

The woman's eyes brightened. "Oh, what kind of wedding?" She seemed oddly excited.

Ruby smiled shyly and said, "Mine."

The woman's eyes widened, and she exclaimed, "Oh, baby, you're in the wrong department! You need to be in the formal dresses."

Ruby felt her cheeks heat up. "No, ma'am," she murmured, glancing down at the rack. "I think this is more my budget."

But the saleslady wouldn't hear of it. She gently took Ruby by the hand and guided her through the store, insisting she follow. Soon, they were in the formal department, and the woman began showing her several dresses, one after another.

She guided Ruby along the racks, her hands brushing over the fabrics as she spoke. "See, something with a fitted waist like this will make you look taller, and the flare at the skirt will move nicely when you walk." She held up a white dress and smiled.

"And this shade of white is just right. You don't need the off-white. You've got a delicate frame, so soft fabrics will flatter you more than anything stiff or heavy."

Ruby watched as the woman pulled a few dresses from the rack, showing her the cuts and textures, describing how each might look in the light at the wedding. She explained which necklines would suit Ruby's shoulders, which lengths would balance her petite frame, and even how certain colors could make her eyes stand out.

Ruby said, "I'm thinking of something with some color."

The lady didn't ask any questions, she just replied, "That sounds wonderful!"

So, she led her to a rack that would normally be for the bridesmaid or a party. Ruby had always loved yellow, so after trying on a few dresses, she picked out a sleeveless, yellow, shift dress. Now she would match the punch and roses. The color reminded her of daffodils that sprang from the dirt near the chicken coop. The dress was simple. No lace but a short train that stopped just at the back of her knees. When she tried it on, it hung like something beautiful.

Patsy looked at Ruby in the mirror. "Girl, you look more delicious than fresh-churned butter on a biscuit."

Ruby giggled. Patsy always had a way with words.

The saleswoman, wearing frosted, pink lipstick came around the corner as Ruby looked at herself in the mirror.

"Well, honey, don't you shine in that color. It was just here waiting on you. Everybody can't wear yellow, but it sure makes you sparkle."

The woman snapped her fingers like she just remembered something important. "Wait here, I have just the thing." She disappeared from the dressing area and shortly returned, holding a white box. Inside was a single strand of pearls.

"These were returned last week, imitation ones, but they are still pretty. Too fussy for most girls these days but perfect with that dress." Ruby reached out hesitantly, picked up the strand, and put them around her neck. They rested just on her collar bone. In that moment, she felt like a real bride.

Ruby paid for the dress and pearls and was walking away from the counter, when the sales lady called out, "What shoes are you wearing with that?"

Ruby hesitated and was ashamed to say, "I have some black ones I can wear."

"Not with that dress, you won't," the lady replied. "Hold on for a minute."

Off through the curtain she went again. It was a long minute as the ceiling fan hummed above her. Ruby investigated the wallet where she'd placed her change, sitting on the edge of the worn bench.

Patsy plopped down beside her, crossing her long legs and letting out a dramatic sigh. "I'm starvin'," she complained, tapping her fingers against her knee. "If I don't get something to eat soon, I'm liable to collapse right here on this bench. Beans, biscuits, a piece of pie—don't care, just feed me!"

Ruby tried not to giggle at her friend's theatrics, though it made the wait feel a little lighter. The woman finally came from behind a door marked EMPLOYEES ONLY and said, "I brought a size six and seven for you to try. You have tiny feet."

She opened the dusty box and revealed a pair of white satin pumps with tiny seed pearls on the toe.

"I'm sorry, but I only have two dollars left. I can't get those shoes," Ruby whispered.

"Yes, you can," the clerk insisted, "they're last season's anyway."

Ruby tried on the shoes reluctantly, and as if magic, the size six were a perfect fit.

"Give me the two dollars and we'll call it even."

The sales lady hadn't asked for her story. She didn't have to. She just looked at Ruby like she was as important as every other customer she had met. That small grace settled into Ruby's bones like a gift from the unknown, and as she walked outside into the sunshine, she smiled.

***

When Ruby and Patsy got home, Ruby placed the wedding dress across the bed and sat the box of pearls and shoes beside it. She couldn't believe she owned such a beautiful dress. She sat on the bed next to it and placed her palms on her knees. So much had happened to her since last March. So many good things had come her way. Her heart was full, but she was still afraid to be happy.

As Ruby was drifting into her thoughts, Mrs. Doyle came in, more excited than if she had been Ruby's mother.

"Let's see what you got, girl!" Ruby grinned and gently pulled the plastic off the dress.

Patsy's mother replied, "You coulda been plain like everyone else but you chose to wear yellow. That color says, 'I have some fight in me, plain and clear. That dress is for someone who wants to be seen.'"

Ruby smiled shyly.

"Mind if I sit?"

Ruby shook her head.

She lowered herself on the bed, dusting the flour off her red apron. "I know you have been through a lot, but you have every right to show up in this world proud. You have become a fine woman, Ruby. Sam is lucky to have you." She gave Ruby a gentle smile and squeezed her knee. As Mrs. Doyle popped up, she announced, "Fried pork chops and applesauce for dinner. Hope you're hungry but not too hungry. Gotta still fit in that dress!"

With that, she walked to the bedroom door and closed it just enough to still let the light through.

***

All the holidays had come and gone, and now it was January sixth. The weather was dreary, a chill cutting through the cannery parking lot and sinking straight into Ruby's bones. This was the most important day in her heart—and the one she dreaded the most. It had arrived too quickly, and Ruby wasn't ready for the ache of missing her daughter's first birthday.

No matter how hard she tried, she couldn't push it out of her mind at work. She boxed tomato cans almost mindlessly, barely registering a word anyone said to her. When her shift finally ended at five, she stepped out of the factory to find Sam sitting at the gate, waiting for her instead of Patsy. Surprised, Ruby ran to him and wrapped her arms tightly around his waist.

"Hold on, Blue Eyes. It's okay. Looks like you had a rough day," Sam said gently.

Ruby's eyes welled with tears, but she didn't want to explain why she felt so heavy inside. "Yeah... I'm just tired," she murmured.

"Let's take a spin," Sam said.

The Bel Air rumbled down the gravel roads, past the Doyle's house and through the southside of Norwood. He turned toward the creek, navigating the bumpy road until they reached a makeshift parking area between two fallen pine trees.

Sam got out and opened the back door, lifting a box and two blankets.

"What's that?" Ruby asked, her curiosity piqued. She hugged herself tighter and shivered. "Sam... I'm freezin' my toes off out here. You sure we couldn't have done this somewhere with walls and heat?"

"Girl, do you have any patience? Come on," he replied, grinning.

Together, they made their way down the embankment. Sam laid a red wool blanket on the ground and motioned for her to sit. Then he sat beside her, draping the extra blanket over both of them. Ruby shivered in more ways than one, unsure what all this careful ceremony was leading to—but she felt, in some quiet way, that it mattered.

Sam sat next to her and opened the box. Inside was a small pink cake with a single candle on top.

"Happy birthday to Lora," Sam said.

Ruby was so shocked, she couldn't speak. She placed her face in her hands and sobbed. After what seemed like forever, Sam wiped her face with his handkerchief and said, "We can't be with her on her first birthday, but we can still celebrate."

"This cake is beautiful, Sam," Ruby commented.

"Yep, I did an excellent job." He smiled, so proud.

Wiping her nose, she exclaimed, "No way. You didn't make this cake."

"I sure did. No box mix either. Of course, I had some help from my sister. I have a lot of skills you don't even know about yet."

With that, he laughed himself silly, and Ruby couldn't help but join him.

"How did you know today was her birthday?" Ruby asked,

"Well," Sam replied dramatically, "you never told me, but maybe a little bird did. Funny how some things fly through the wind and land just where they need to. Now, let's celebrate and eat cake—except I've got one problem," he said with a grin. "I didn't bring forks."

They both burst into laughter, the sound echoing across the quiet clearing.

CHAPTER TWENTY-THREE

DEVIL'S ELBOW

Sam hesitated outside Patsy's house, his jaw clenched tight, before he gave in and climbed into the back seat beside Ruby. Jim was determined to drive that night even though it wasn't his car and he'd had a drink or two at the pool hall before they picked up Ruby. Jim had the window down, with a cigarette burning full. Jim and Marsha had been dating a couple of months, but Sam wasn't real keen on him.

"A little brash and hot headed," Sam had commented.

Martha didn't see anything but a real Army man in a cowboy hat. Jim had to be back at Fort Leonard Wood by nine p.m. He had missed the bus from Ava and talked Sam into taking him back. Ruby came along for the ride, even if it meant staying out so late on a work night. Jim stayed behind the wheel, smug, knuckles loose on the steering wheel. Martha, giggling in the passenger seat, twirled her hair and leaned into him like nothing in the world could touch them.

Jim wasn't a cowboy, just a twenty-three year old with a bad attitude and bad skin and a six pack of Falstaff under the seat. Martha sat making googly eyes next to him like he was John Wayne.

The car headed north on Highway 13, that cursed stretch of road Ruby had never trusted. It twisted through the hills like a snake, silent and watching. Too many tragedies here. Too many lives gone still under the trees. But she told herself not to think about it. Not tonight. The only light around was from the moon peeking out of the clouds.

The radio fizzled to life: "Green Onions," a simple, instrumental tune. Martha whooped and danced in her seat, curls bouncin' every time Jim hit a bump in the road, her laughter cutting through the thick Ozark dark like a firework too close to the ground. Jim sped up, tires whispering along the blacktop. Ruby stared out the window, the trees blurring past like shadows that didn't want to be seen.

They blew through Springfield just as the lights began to bloom along the roadside. For a brief moment, Ruby let herself imagine living there. A little house. A quiet life. Maybe. But not really. She and Sam had bigger dreams. Lincoln, Nebraska. A clean start, far from these hills with their long memories and restless dead.

Then the song changed.

Moon River... Soft. Haunting. The notes drifted through the car like a memory that didn't belong to anyone. Ruby's breath caught. A slow ache rose in her chest. Tears pressed behind her eyes without reason. Something about that melody made her immediately sad. She didn't have any reason to be sad anymore, but the haunting ache of her past sometimes came back and rolled in like an April thunderstorm. The music made her uneasy, like the calm just before a tornado. All still and peaceful and deceiving. Like a lullaby that wouldn't let you sleep.

I'm crossin' you...

"I hate this road," she whispered, teeth clenched.

Sam slid his arm around her and gave her a kiss on the cheek, whispering, "It's okay, baby. He's foolish but he ain't no fool."

Jim popped open a beer, causing the foam to dribble out of the opening.

Ruby was confused. Something was bad off, but she didn't remember dreamin' about it, did she? She needed her dream book to confirm whether that was true or not.

She pressed closer into Sam, clutching his flannel arm around her. Ruby didn't want to be in that car anymore.

She cried, "Sam, make him slow down!"

Dream maker...

Up front, Jim laughed, reckless, cigarette dangling, beer in one hand, he pulled Martha against him, his other hand barely holding the wheel. The road curved hard beneath them. His cigarette flared, then dropped—fire in his lap. Jim jumped and slapped at the ember, while Martha laughed hysterically.

Sam lunged forward, voice sharp. "Damn it, Jim, pull over now!

Two drifters...

But Jim didn't stop or slow down. He couldn't. Or wouldn't.

Just as the car topped the hill and the road cut hard left, Jim crossed the yellow line and drove straight into the oncoming car.

CHAPTER TWENTY-FOUR

FADE TO LIGHT

The cold settled over the hills like a heavy coat, thick and stubborn. February cold was a different kind of cruel, not sharp and biting like January but slow and seeping, the kind that worked its way into bone and breath without warning. The sky hung low and black, not a single star breaking through the clouds.

The air smelled of oil and burning rubber. Porch lights flickered weakly in the distance, casting tired halos that didn't reach the road. Time felt like it stopped. Like the world was holding its breath. Waiting for something it didn't want to see. The old timers would say the darker the night, the closer the fox was to the henhouse. This fox was indeed in the henhouse.

Highway 13, the Devil's Elbow, twisted like a snake with no conscious. A piece of road complained about for years, lives scattered like confetti. Ordinary things turned into shards of tragedy. Ruby lay in the road, her chest rose once, then stopped. Eyes wide, staring at something no one else could see. The sheriff knelt beside her, head bowed, hat in hand, red and blue lights flashing over her face in an oddly patriotic cast. America's colors shing down on a girl who never got her fair share of freedom.

She felt the heaviness in her chest and thought about all those Cracker Jack boxes she'd torn open as a girl. Hoping for a prize she never got. Then it hit her, the popcorn itself had been the prize all along. Little sweet bits, tiny joys, the first birthday cake, Aunt Lena's sweet smile. That was what mattered. She'd been looking for something big and shiny, but it had been there all along in the small things she had always overlooked. No pain, just hush. Then a sound, not loud but clean. Like a magnificent harp, pure and golden. Rising from the mountains, it didn't hurt her ears, just opened a memory she hadn't realized she had forgotten. The shadows raised their heads.

And then, as her breath thinned, the world before her began to shift. It was as if an old movie reel had started to play—flickering light against the dark. She saw a baby with a dimpled chin, a little girl running through a field of jonquils, her laughter bright as bells. The pictures moved faster: an older woman with silver in her hair, children gathered around her knees, then those children growing, scattering like seeds into their own lives.

And in that moment, Ruby understood: This wasn't the end of her story—it was only the beginning.

Epilogue

For years, everyone whispered that the Pontiac driver had been drunk, that the wreck was all their fault. The Amsler family held onto that story like a talisman, handing it down through generations. At church pews, the diner counter, the post office line, they'd nod and murmur, "Wasn't their fault... that other car was full of college kids, drunk, speeding." It dulled the sharp edge of grief, a small relief against the unbearable truth: A tragedy had stolen their daughter. In a town where sorrow quickly became gossip, that version was easier to live with.

But the highway records told another story. Both cars were speeding. A patrolman had clocked the Pontiac at over eighty and was in pursuit when he heard the crash. The Chevy veered into the oncoming car. Seven lives ended in an instant. The official reports were clear.

After the wreck, Ruby became something else—something spotless. The family spoke of her in hushed voices, as if she'd always been perfect. They told anyone who'd listen that she was kind, brilliant, beloved. That Sam adored her, and she him. That she had a bright future, her yellow wedding dress still laid out on the bed. Some of it was true, but much of it had been rewritten in the haze of grief and guilt.

No one spoke of the years before: the silences, the punishments, the shame piled on her shoulders. They never mentioned how they'd sent her away or how she carried blame that wasn't hers. They erased her name from family secrets. It was easier to pretend she had always been good, always loved. Mourning was cleaner when the dead were saints. So, Ruby became one—polished, posthumous, not the girl she was but the girl they needed her to be.

Jim was the only one who walked away. He left the Ozarks and never returned. Until his death in 2010, he retold the story of that night—said only the cold saved him, that he'd been in the backseat, not behind the wheel.

Devil's Elbow, the curve that took them all, still winds through the trees. A new highway runs nearby, but every spring, wildflowers bloom along the old road—unnaturally bright, mysteriously placed. They return year after year, like memory refusing to fade.

In a forgotten Ozarks cemetery, beneath whispering pine and pale sycamore, three souls lie side by side—Sam, Ruby, and Martha—bound beneath a single stone. Around them rest generations of Sam's people, their names fading beneath moss and rain. Theirs is a plain marker, the letters carved deep but spare, joined forever by the same cruel day. Only one touch of grace breaks the stone's simplicity—a single jonquil etched beside Ruby's name.

A narrow river runs close by, its waters rising each winter until the road disappears beneath the flood. For weeks, no one can reach the cemetery, and the hill stands alone—quiet, untouched, holding its secrets close.

Those who find the place say it feels different from the rest of the valley—still, almost tender. Some swear the wind softens there, as if careful not to wake them. Others say it's the quietest spot in the county and that peace settled there long ago and never left.

Acknowledgements

Thanks to my husband, who raised himself while my face was stuck in a computer. To my five beautiful and precious children—Brandy, Bryan, Bailey, Brandy Michelle, and Brianna—each one a miracle and a light in my life. To my six precious grandbabies—Braxton, Gavin, Braylee, Annabelle, Tucker, and Blaise—who made me a Bee Bee, filled my world with happiness, and motivated me to find their truth. To my bonus sons Robert and Zack who steadfastly love my girls. And to my family, who loved me fiercely, even though they didn't have to.

My deepest thanks to Jana, my loyal friend and travel partner, who listened to every detail without complaint. For my beta readers, Carrie, Stephanie, Brianna, Lisa, Judy, and Heather, who gave me the best advice and ignored my typos. Many thanks to my editor, Marni MacRae.

I am forever grateful to those who shared the hard, hidden truths so Ruby could finally step into the light. This story holds the voices of my mother and all the angels before me, whose pain and resilience gave it power. I honor the family I discovered along the way and those who helped me piece together the truth—especially Judy, Carla, Muriel, Ernest, Terry, Lloyd, David, Clyde, Paul, and Stephanie, for answering painful questions with grace. And finally, for Ruby, who showed the ultimate courage by loving me enough to break the cycle.

www.ingramcontent.com/pod-product-compliance
Lightning Source LLC
LaVergne TN
LVHW042251070526
838201LV00110B/330/J